Massachusetts Historical Society

Tribute of the Massachusetts Historical Society

Massachusetts Historical Society

Tribute of the Massachusetts Historical Society

ISBN/EAN: 9783744664318

Printed in Europe, USA, Canada, Australia, Japan

Cover: Foto ©ninafisch / pixelio.de

More available books at **www.hansebooks.com**

TRIBUTE

OF THE

MASSACHUSETTS HISTORICAL SOCIETY.

To the Memory

OF

EDWARD EVERETT,

JANUARY 30, 1865.

・ー●●ー・

BOSTON:

MASSACHUSETTS HISTORICAL SOCIETY.

1865.

TRIBUTE

MASSACHUSETTS HISTORICAL SOCIETY.

A SPECIAL Meeting of the Massachusetts Historical Society was
held in the Dowse Library on Monday evening, January 30,
1865, to commemorate their late illustrious associate, Edward
Everett. The attendance was very large.

. The meeting was called to order at 7½ o'clock by the President,
the Hon. Robert C. Winthrop, who spoke as follows : —

GENTLEMEN OF THE MASSACHUSETTS HISTORICAL SOCIETY:

The occasion of this meeting is but too well known to
you all. None of us were strangers to the grief which
pervaded this community on the recent announcement of
the death of Edward Everett. Not a few of us have had
the privilege of uniting with the public authorities, who
hastened to assume the whole charge of his funeral, in
paying the last tribute to his honored remains. And
more than one of us have already had an opportunity of
giving some feeble expression to our sense of the loss
which has been sustained by our city, our Commonwealth, and our whole country.

But we are here this evening to take up the theme
again somewhat more deliberately, as a Society of which

he was so long one of the most valuable, as well as one
of the most distinguished members. We are here not
merely to unite in lamenting the close of a career which
has been crowded with so many good words and good
works for the community and the country at large, but
to give utterance to our own particular sorrow for the
breach which has been made in our own cherished circle.

Mr. Everett was elected a member of this Society on
the 27th of April, 1820, when he was but twenty-six
years of age; and, at the time of his death, his name
stood second in order of seniority on the roll of our
resident members. I need not attempt to say to you how
much we have prized his companionship, how often we
have profited of his counsels, or how deeply we have been
indebted to him for substantial services which no one
else could have rendered so well.

His earliest considerable effort in our behalf was a lecture delivered before us on the 31st of October, 1833. It
was entitled " Anecdotes of Early Local History," and will
be found in the second volume of his collected works, —
now lying upon our table, — with an extended note or
appendix containing many interesting details concerning
the Society, its objects and its members. But it is only
within the last nine or ten years, and since his public life —
so far as office is necessary to constitute public life — was
brought to a close, that he has been in the way of taking
an active part in our proceedings. No one can enter the
room in which we are gathered without remembering how
frequently, during that period, his voice has been heard
among us in rendering such honors to others, as now,

alas, we are so unexpectedly called to pay to himself. No
one can forget his admirable tributes to the beloved Pres-
cott, to the excellent Nathan Hale, to the venerated
Quincy, among our immediate associates ; — to Daniel D.
Barnard of Albany and Henry D. Gilpin of Philadelphia,
to Washington Irving, to Hallam, to Humboldt, to Macaulay, among our domestic and foreign honorary members.

Still less will any one be likely to forget the noble
eulogy which he pronounced, at our request, on the 9th
of December, 1858, upon that remarkable self-made man
whom we have ever delighted to honor as our largest
benefactor, and in whose pictured presence we are at this
moment assembled. Often as I have listened to our lamented friend, since the year 1824, — when I followed
him with at least one other whom I see before me to
Plymouth Rock, and heard his splendid discourse on the
Pilgrim Fathers, — I can hardly recall anything of his,
more striking of its kind, or more characteristic of its
author, than that elaborate delineation of the life of
Thomas Dowse. No one, certainly, who was present on
the occasion, can fail to recall the exhibition which he
gave us, in its delivery, of the grasp and precision of his
wonderful memory, — when in describing the collection
of water colors, now in the Athenæum gallery. which was
the earliest of Mr. Dowse's possessions, he repeated,
without faltering, the unfamiliar names of more than
thirty of the old masters from whose works they were
copied, and then turning at once to the description of
the library itself, as we see it now around us, proceeded
to recite the names of fifty-three of the ancient authors

of Greek and Roman literature, of nineteen of the modern
German, of fourteen of the Italian, of forty-seven of the
French, of sixteen or seventeen of the Portuguese and
Spanish, making up in all an aggregate of more than one
hundred and eighty names of artists and authors, many of
them as hard to pronounce as they were difficult to be
remembered, but which he rehearsed, without the aid of
a note and without the hesitation of an instant, with as
much ease and fluency as he doubtless had rolled off
the famous catalogue of the ships, in the second book of
Homer's Iliad, with the text-book in his hand, as a college student or as Greek professor, half a century before!

I need hardly add that with this library, now our most
valued treasure, the name of Mr. Everett will henceforth
be hardly less identified than that of Mr. Dowse himself.
Indeed, he had been associated with it long before it was
so munificently transferred to us. By placing yonder portrait of him, taken in his earliest manhood, upon the
walls of the humble apartment in which the books were
originally collected, — the only portrait ever admitted to
their companionship, — our worthy benefactor seems himself to have designated Edward Everett as the presiding
genius or patron saint of this library; and as such he will
be enshrined by us, and by all who shall succeed us, as
long as the precious books and the not less precious
canvas shall escape the ravages of time.

I may not omit to remind you that our lamented friend
— who was rarely without some labor of love for others
in prospect — had at least two matters in hand for us
at the time of his death, which he was hoping, and which

we all were hoping, that he would soon be able to complete. One of them was a memoir of that noble patriot of South Carolina, James Louis Petigru, whose lifelong devotion to the cause of the American Union, alike in the days of nullification and of secession, will secure him the grateful remembrance of all to whom that Union is dear. The other was a volume of Washington's private letters, which he was preparing to publish in our current series of historical collections. It is hardly a month since he told me that the letters were all copied, and that he was sorry to be obliged to postpone the printing of them a little longer, in order to find time for the annotations with which he desired to accompany them.

But you do not require to be told, gentlemen, that what Mr. Everett has done, or has proposed to do, specifically for our own Society, would constitute a very small part of all that he has accomplished in that cause of American history in which we are associated. It is true that he has composed no independent historical work, nor ever published any volume of biography more considerable than the excellent memoir of Washington, which he prepared, at the suggestion of his friend Lord Macaulay, for the new edition of the Encyclopædia Britannica. But there is no great epoch, — there is hardly a single great event, — of our national or of our colonial history, which he has not carefully depicted and brilliantly illustrated in his occasional discourses. I have sometimes thought that no more attractive or more instructive history of our country could be presented to the youth of our land, than is found in the series of anniversary orations which he has delivered during the last forty years. Collect those orations into a volume by themselves; arrange them in their historical order: " The First Settlement of New England," " The Settlement of Massachusetts," " The Battle of Bloody Brook in King Philip's War," " The Seven Years' War, the School of the Revolution," " The First Battles of the Revolutionary War," " The Battle of Lexington," " The Battle of Bunker Hill," " Dorchester in 1630, 1776, and 1855;" combine with them those " Anecdotes of Early Local History," which he prepared for our own Society, and add to them his charming discourses on " The Youth of Washington," and " The Character of Washington," on " The Boyhood and the Early Days of Franklin," and his memorable eulogies on Adams and Jefferson, on Lafayette, on John Quincy Adams and on Daniel Webster, and I know not in what other volume the young men, or even the old men, of our land could find the history of the glorious past more accurately or more admirably portrayed. I know not where they could find the toils and trials and struggles of our colonial or revolutionary fathers set forth with greater fulness of detail or greater felicity of illustration. As one reads those orations and discourses at this moment, they might almost be regarded as successive chapters of a continuous and comprehensive work which had been composed and recited on our great national anniversaries, just as the chapters of Herodotus are said to have been recited at the Olympic festivals of ancient Greece.

Undoubtedly, however, it is rather as an actor and an

orator in some of the later scenes of our country's history, than as an author, that Mr. Everett will be longest remembered. Indeed, since he first entered on the stage of mature life, there has hardly been a scene of any sort in that great historic drama, which of late, alas, has assumed the most terrible form of tragedy, in which he has not been called to play a more or less conspicuous part; and we all know how perfectly every part which has been assigned him has been performed. If we follow him from the hour when he left the University of Cambridge, with the highest academic honors, at an age when so many others are hardly prepared to enter there, down to the fatal day when he uttered those last impressive words at Faneuil Hall, we shall find him everywhere occupied with the highest duties, and everywhere discharging those duties with consummate ability and unwearied devotion. Varied and brilliant accomplishments, laborious research, copious diction, marvellous memory, magnificent rhetoric, a gracious presence, a glorious voice, an ardent patriotism controlling his public career, an unsullied purity crowning his private life, — what element was there wanting in him for the complete embodiment of the classic orator, as Cato and Quinctilian so tersely and yet so comprehensively defined him eighteen hundred years ago — " *Vir bonus, dicendi peritus!* "

But I may not occupy more of your time in these introductory remarks, intended only to exhibit our departed friend in his relations to our own Society, and to open the way for those who are prepared to do better

justice to his general career and character. Let me
only add that our Standing Committee have requested our
associates, Mr. Hillard and Dr. Lothrop, to prepare some
appropriate resolutions for the occasion, and that the
Society is now ready to receive them.

Mr. Hillard then proceeded as follows : —

The Psalmist says, " The days of our years are threescore years and ten, and if by reason of strength they be
forescore years, yet is their strength labor and sorrow."
The latter part of this sentence is not altogether true ; at
least, it is not without exceptions as numerous as the
rule. To say nothing of the living, we who have witnessed the serene and beautiful old age of Quincy, protracted more than twenty years after threescore years and
ten, will not admit that all of life beyond that limit is of
necessity " labor and sorrow." But in these words there
is much of truth as this, that he who has lived to be
threescore and ten years old should feel that he has had
his fair share of life, and if any more years are dropped
into his lap he must receive them as a gift not promised
at his birth. And thus no man who dies after the age of
seventy can be said to have died unseasonably or prema-
turely. But the shock with which the news of Mr.
Everett's death fell upon the community was due to its
unexpectedness as well as its suddenness. We knew
that he was an old man, but we did not feel that he was
such. There was nothing either in his aspect or his life
that warned us of departure or reminded us of decay.
His powers were so vigorous, his industry was so great,

his sympathies were so active, his eloquence was so rich and glowing, his elocution still so admirable, that he appeared before us as a man in the very prime of life, and when he died it was as if the sun had gone down at noon. The impression made by his death was the highest tribute that could be paid to the worth of his life.

In 1819, after an absence of nearly five years, Mr. Everett returned from Europe at the age of twenty-five, the most finished and accomplished man that had been seen in New England, and it will be generally admitted that he maintained this superiority to the last. From that year down to the hour of his death he was constantly before the public eye, and never without a marked and peculiar influence upon the community, especially upon students and scholars. You and I, Mr. President, are old enough to have come under the spell of the magician at that early period of his life, when he presented the most attractive combination of graceful and blooming youth with mature intellectual power. The young man of to-day, familiar with that expression of gravity, almost of sadness, which his countenance has habitually worn of late, can hardly imagine what he then was, when his " bosom's lord sat light upon his throne," when the winds of hope filled his sails, and his looks and movements were informed with a spirit of morning freshness and vernal promise.

In the forty-five years which passed between his return home and his death, Mr. Everett's industry was untiring, and the amount of work he accomplished was immense. What he published would alone entitle him to the praise of a very industrious man, but this forms but a part of his labors. Of what has been called the master-vice of sloth he knew nothing. He was independent of the amusements and relaxations which most hard-working men interpose between their hours of toil. He was always in harness.

Some persons have regretted that he gave so much time to merely occasional productions, instead of devoting himself to some one great work ; but without speculating upon the comparative value of what we have and what we might have had, it is enough to say that with his genius and temperament on the one hand, and our institutions and form of society on the other, it was a sort of necessity that his mind should have taken the direction that it did. For he was the child of his time, and was always in harmony with the spirit of the age and country in which his lot was cast. He was pre-eminently rich in the fruits of European culture ; Greece, Rome, England, France, Italy, and Germany, all helped by liberal contributions to swell his stores of intellectual wealth, but yet no man was ever more national in feeling, more patriotic in motive and impulse, more thoroughly American in grain and fibre. Loving books as he did, he would yet have pined and languished if he had been doomed to live in the unsympathetic air of a great library. The presence, the comprehension, the sympathy of his kind were as necessary to him as his daily bread.

"Two words," says Macaulay, "form the key of the Baconian doctrine, Utility and Progress." I think these two words also go far to reveal and interpret Mr.

Everett's motives and character. Not that he did not seek honorable distinction, not that he did not take pleasure in the applause which he had fairly earned; but stronger even than these propelling impulses was his desire to be of service to his fellowmen, to do good in his day and generation. He loved his country with a fervid love, and he loved his race with a generous and comprehensive philanthropy. He was always ready to work cheerfully in any direction when he thought he could do any good, though the labor might not be particularly congenial to his tastes, and would not add anything to his literary reputation. The themes which he handled, during his long life of intellectual action, were very various, they were treated with great affluence of learning, singular beauty of illustration, and elaborate and exquisite harmony of style, but always in such a way as to bear practical fruit, and contribute to the advancement of society and the elevation of humanity.

So, too, Mr. Everett was a sincere and consistent friend of progress. He was, it is true, conservative in his instincts and convictions; I mean in a large and liberal, and not in a narrow and technical sense. But that he was an extreme conservative, or that he valued an institution simply because it was old, is not only not true, but, I think, the reverse of truth. He had a distaste to extreme views of any kind, and by the constitution of his mind, was disposed to take that middle ground which partisan zeal is prone to identify with timidity or indifference. But he was a man of generous impulses and large sympathies. No one was more quick to recognize true progress, and greet it with a more hospitable welcome. No man of his age would have more readily and heartily acknowledged the many points in which the world has advanced since he was young.

It would not be seasonable here to dwell upon Mr. Everett's public or political career, but I may be permitted to add that I think he had a genuine faith in the institutions of his country, which did not grow fainter as he grew older. He believed in man's capacity for self-government, and had confidence in popular instincts. He was fastidious in his social tastes, but not aristocratic; that is, if he preferred one man to another it was for essential and not adventitious qualities, for what they were, and not for what they had. He was uniformly kind to the young, and always prompt to recognize and encourage merit in a young person.

Mr. Everett, if not the founder of the school of American deliberative eloquence, was its most brilliant representative. In his orations and occasional discourses will be found his best title to remembrance, and by them his name will surely be transmitted to future generations. In judging of them, we must bear in mind that the aim of the deliberative orator is to treat a subject in such a way as to secure and fix the attention of a popular audience, and this aim Mr. Everett never lost sight of. If it be said that his discourses are not marked by originality of construction, or philosophical depth of thought, it may be replied that had they been so, they would have been less attractive to his hearers. They are remarkable for a combination of qualities rarely, if ever before, so happily blended, and especially for the grace, skill, and tact with which the resources of the widest cultivation are so used as to instruct the common mind and touch the common heart. For, whatever were the subject, Mr. Everett always took his audience along with him, from first to last. He never soared or wandered out of their sight.

I need not dwell upon the singular beauty and finish of his elocution. Those who have heard him speak will need no description of the peculiar charm and grace of his manner, and no description will give any adequate impression of it to those who never heard him. It was a manner easily caricatured but not easily imitated. His power over an audience remained unimpaired to the last. At the age of seventy he spoke with all the animation of youth, and easily filled the largest hall with that rich and flexible voice, the tones of which time had hardly touched.

His organization was delicate and refined, his temperament was sensitive and sympathetic. The opinion of those whom he loved and esteemed was weighty with him. Praise was ever cordial to him, and more necessary than to most men who had achieved such high and assured distinction. Doubtful as the statement may seem to those who knew him but slightly, or only saw him on the platform with his " robes and singing garlands " about him, he was to the last a modest and self-distrustful man. He never appeared in public without a slight flutter of apprehension lest he should fall short of that 'standard which he had created for himself. His want of self-confidence, and, in later years, his want of animal spirits, sometimes produced a coldness of manner, which, by superficial observers, was set down to coldness of heart, but most unjustly.

His nature was courteous, gentle, and sweet. Few men were ever more worthy than he to wear " the grand old name of gentleman." His manners were graceful, more scholarly than is usual with men who had been so much in public life as he had been, and sometimes covered with a delicate veil of reserve. Conflict and contest were distasteful to him, and it was his disposition to follow the things that make for peace. He had a true respect for the intellectual rights of others, and it was no fault of his if he ever lost a friend through difference of opinion.

Permit me to turn for a moment to Mr. Everett's public life for an illustration of his character. In forensic contests, sarcasm and invective are formidable and frequent weapons. The House of Commons quailed before the younger Pitt's terrible powers of sarcasm. An eminent living statesman and orator of Great Britain is remarkable for both these qualities. But neither invective nor sarcasm is to be found in Mr. Everett's speeches. I think this absence is to be ascribed not to an intellectual want but to a moral grace.

Great men, public men, have also their inner and private life, and sometimes this must be thrown by the

honest painter into shadow. But in Mr. Everett's case
there was no need of this, for his private life was spotless.
In conduct and conversation he always conformed to
the highest standard which public opinion exacts of
the members of that profession to which he originally
belonged. As a brother, husband, father, and friend,
there was no duty that he did not discharge, no call that
he did not obey. He was generous in giving, and equally
generous in sacrificing. Where he was most known
he was best loved. He was wholly free from that
exacting temper in small things which men, eminent
and otherwise estimable, sometimes fall into. His daily
life was made beautiful by a pervading spirit of thoughtful consideration for those who stood nearest to him.
His household manners were delightful, and his household discourse was brightened by a lambent play of wit
and humor; qualities which he possessed in no common
measure, though they were rarely displayed before the
public. Could the innermost circle of Mr. Everett's life
be revealed to the general eye, it could not fail to deepen
the sense of bereavement which his death has awakened,
and to increase the reverence with which his memory is
and will be cherished.

No man ever bore his faculties and his eminence
more meekly than he. He never declined the lowly
and commonplace duties of life. He was always ap-
proachable and accessible. The constant and various
interruptions to which he was exposed by the innu-
merable calls made upon his time and thoughts were
borne by him with singular patience and sweetness.

His industry was as methodical as it was uniform. However busy he might be, he could always find time for any service which a friend required at his hands. He was scrupulously faithful and exact in small things. He never broke an appointment or a promise. His splendid powers worked with all the regularity and precision of the most nicely adjusted machinery. If he had undertaken to have a discourse, a report, an article, ready at a certain time, it might be depended upon as surely as the rising of the sun.

I feel that I have hardly touched upon the remarkable qualities of Mr. Everett's mind and character, and yet I have occupied as much of your time as is becoming. I have only to offer a few resolutions, in which I have endeavored briefly and simply to give expression to what we all feel.

Mr. Hillard then presented the following resolutions : —

Resolved, That as members of the Massachusetts Historical Society, we record, with mingled pride and sorrow, our sense of what we have lost in the death of our late illustrious associate, Edward Everett, the wise statesman, the eloquent orator, the devoted patriot, the finished scholar, whose long life of singular and unbroken intellectual activity has shed new lustre upon the name of our country in every part of the civilized world, and whose noble powers and unrivalled accomplishments were always inspired by an enlarged and enlightened philanthropy, and dedicated to the best interests of knowledge, virtue, and truth.

Resolved, That we recall with peculiar sensibility the personal qualities and private virtues of our departed friend, the purity and beauty of his daily life, his strict allegiance to duty, the strength and tenderness of his domestic affections, the uniform conscientiousness which regulated his conduct, his spirit of self-sacrifice, his thoughtful consideration for the rights and happiness of others, and the gentleness with which his great faculties and high honors were borne.

Resolved, That the President of the Society be requested to transmit these resolutions to the family of our lamented associate, with an expression of our deep sympathy with them in their loss, and of our trust that they may find consolation not merely in the remembrance of his long, useful, and illustrious career, but in the hopes and promises of that religion of which he was a firm believer, and which was ever to him a staff of support through life.

The resolutions were seconded by the Rev. Dr. Lothrop, who then addressed the meeting, as follows : —

MR. PRESIDENT : I rise, at your request and at that of the standing committee, to second the resolutions which have just been offered, and to pay my portion of the tribute of profound, grateful, and affectionate respect, which the Society would offer this evening to the memory of our eminent deceased associate. And as we gather within these walls and in this room, where we have so often welcomed his presence, I feel brought back upon me afresh that sense of loneliness and of personal bereavement, which, in

common with so many, I had when I first heard that one
who for more than forty years had been the object of my
youthful and my mature admiration, one whose speech
never disappointed me, but had often stirred my heart
with pure and noble emotions, and to whom I and others
had so long been accustomed to turn upon all occasions of
public interest and importance, as the person who could
do and say, in the best way, the best things to be done and
said, was really dead, and that the utterances of his wisdom and eloquence would never more be heard by us on
earth. My sorrow, however, at his departure, the sorrow
of all of us, I think, must be greatly softened by the
extraordinary felicity of the time and manner of his death,
and by the recollection of the grand and noble career of
which that death was the close.

In view of my profession and the pulpit which it has
been my honor and happiness to occupy in this city, it
may be permitted me, in glancing at his career, to speak
with some particularity of that which was the beginning
of it before the public — his brief but honorable connection with the clerical profession, and his short but brilliant
pastorate at Brattle Street Church. Mr. Everett has said,
I believe, that on leaving college his strongest preferences
were for the law; but the influence and advice of friends,
combining with the promptings of his own heart, the deep
religious instincts of his nature, determined his choice of
the Christian ministry. That determination must now be
regarded as fortunate for him and for us. He left the
pulpit, indeed, shortly after he had entered it; but no
true man ever forgets that he has stood in it, and the

studies, the spiritual discipline and culture of his early
profession seem to me to have exerted upon Mr. Everett's
mind and heart blessed and important influences, which
affected his whole subsequent career, and impregnated his
life and character with the simple but grand dignity of
purity. Graduating in 1811, at the age of seventeen, he
spent two years and a few months at Cambridge, pursuing
theological studies, and discharging at the same time the
onerous duties of a tutorship. On the 10th of December,
1813, a mere youth, who had not yet numbered twenty
winters, he first stood in Brattle Street pulpit to preach
as a candidate. Fame had preceded him, and told of his
talents rich and rare, of his great learning and his great
capacity to learn, — marvellous even then in the judgment
of his peers and of the University, — of his extraordinary
gift of golden speech, his powers of winning, persuasive
oratory.

The great, though vague and undefined expectations
thus awakened, were not disappointed. I have been told
by many who distinctly remember the occasion, that when
he rose in the pulpit that morning, a youthful modesty,
almost timidity, blending with the dignity which a grave
and reverent sense of the importance of his office inspired,
lent a fascinating charm to his manner, and that from the
moment he opened his lips, the audience were held spell-
bound to the end of the service. When the days of his
engagement were numbered, the universal cry was,
" Come unto us in the name of the Lord ; break unto us
the bread of life, and let all these rich gifts find their
usefulness and their glory in the service of the Master

3

here among us." He heard the cry as the leadings of Providence, and came. His ordination, on the 9th of February, 1814, was an occasion of as deep interest as any event of the kind ever excited. The most eminent and excellent men-of that day took part in it. It brought a perfect satisfaction to the people. It awakened the most brilliant anticipations. It was accompanied not simply with the hope, but with the conviction, that the former glory of that pulpit, which the death of Buckminster had veiled for a season, would be revived with increased and increasing splendor. That conviction was verified. As the months rolled on, Brattle Street Church, then near the residences rather than the business of the people, was crowded Sunday after Sunday with audiences of the intelligent and the cultivated, who went away charmed, instructed, religiously impressed; and the records of the communion show that it was a season of spiritual growth as well as of outward prosperity. But the year had not reached its close before painful rumors began to prevail that this was not to last, and at the end of thirteen months after his ordination, he resigned his charge, to accept the Eliot Professorship of Greek Literature in the University at Cambridge, to which he had been appointed by the corporation, with leave of study and travel for five years in Europe, in further preparation for its duties.

He left the clerical profession, and virtually the pulpit, when he thus left Brattle Street Church. On his return from Europe, indeed, and for two or three years subsequently, he preached occasionally, some ten or fifteen,

perhaps twenty times in all. I may be permitted a brief
allusion to some of these occasions, which I remember.
First, of course, he preached in what had been his own
pulpit, Brattle Street, in the summer of 1819, a few weeks
after his return. I was one of the mighty company that
thronged the aisles of that church on that day, and, standing on the window-seat nearest the door in the north
gallery, heard him for the first time when I was just old
enough to receive my first idea of eloquence, to understand
and feel something of its power. A month or two later,
in December of that year, I think, he preached a famous
Christmas sermon at King's Chapel, and on the first Sunday in December, 1820, the Quarterly Charity Lecture, at
the Old South Church, which was crowded to overflowing
to hear him. Another memorable and impressive sermon
of his, preached several times in different pulpits in this
vicinity, and which several gentlemen present must distinctly remember, was on the text, " The time is short."
He preached the sermon at the funeral of the Rev. Dr.
Bentley, of Salem, on the 3d of January, 1820, President
Kirkland and Dr. Ware of the University officiating in
the other parts of the service. This arrangement was
probably made in the expectation that Dr. Bentley had left
his valuable library to Harvard College. But the doc-
torate from Cambridge was conferred too late, and it was
found that the library had been bequeathed to Alleghany
College; so, to the deep regret of those who heard it,
Mr. Everett's sermon on this occasion was never published. On the 19th of January, 1821, he preached the
sermon at the dedication of the First Congregational

Church in the city of New York, of which the late Rev. William Ware subsequently became pastor. This sermon was published, and is, I believe, the only sermon he ever published. It is the only one I have ever seen. In style it is simple and grave, less rhetorical than his orations. It is liberal, but conservative, in its theology, broad and catholic in its charity, fervent in tone and spirit, evidently the product of a devout heart. This dedication at New York was the last or among the last occasions on which he preached. I feel quite confident that he did not preach after 1821, because the next year, as some who hear me will remember, in addition to the lectures connected with his professorship, and other duties at Cambridge, he was occupied with a course of lectures, whose preparation, judging from their learning and brilliancy, must have cost him no little time and study, on Art and Architecture, — more especially, if my memory serves me, on Greek and Egyptian Architecture, — which he delivered at what was then called the Pantheon Hall, on Washington Street, a little south of the Boylston Market. Lectures of this kind were then unusual in Boston, and these, having in addition to their novelty the strong attraction of the name and fame of the lecturer, were attended by an audience as cultivated and appreciative as ever assembled for a similar purpose.

From this review it appears that his whole connection with the pulpit, including his preparatory studies and pastorate, before he went to Europe, and the period during which he preached occasionally after his return, was only about five years. His exclusive connection

with it as pastor was only one year and a month lacking
four days, from the 9th of February, 1814, to the 5th
of March, 1815. In this brief period he made an
impression, as a preacher, which abides distinct and
clear to this hour in many hearts. He left the pulpit
with the reputation of being the most eminent and
eloquent man in it; and he left in and with the profession one book — his " Defence of Christianity " —
which at the time it was published was justly regarded
as one of the most learned and important theological
works that had then been written in America, and which,
considering its contents, the circumstances under which
it was prepared, and the extreme youth of the author,
may still be regarded as one of the most extraordinary
books produced at any time in any profession. It is
one of those books, of which the paradox may be uttered,
that its success caused its failure. It so perfectly
accomplished its work that it almost dropt out of existence. Few of the present generation ever heard of it,
fewer still know anything about it. Copies of it can
now be found only here and there, on the shelves of
Public Libraries, or among the books of aged clergymen.
It was prepared, as some gentlemen here will remember,
in reply to a work by Mr. George Bethune English,
who graduated at Cambridge in 1807, the year Mr.
Everett entered. This gentleman, not without talents,
but erratic in his career, which his death terminated in
1828, remained at Cambridge four or five years after
graduating, studied theology, and I believe, preached
for a brief period. Being led, apparently by the study

of the deistical works of Anthony Collins, to adopt opinions unfavorable to Christianity as a divine revelation, he published a book entitled, " The Grounds of Christianity Examined by Comparing the New Testament with the Old." This work, plausible in spirit, having the appearance of great candor in statement and fairness in argument, attracted attention and was much read. It unsettled the faith of many, and, if left unanswered, seemed destined to do this for many more.

Mr. Everett did, what several older men, I have heard, attempted without success; he made a triumphant answer to Mr. English's book, in a volume of nearly five hundred pages, which to this day must be regarded as replete with the learning bearing upon its particular point. Cogent in argument, clear and close in its reasoning, eloquent often in the fervor and glow of a devout faith, keen yet kind in its wit and satire, conclusive in its exposition of the ignorance of his opponent, his plagiarism, and his dishonesty in the use of his materials, this book so completely extinguished Mr. English and his disciples, that it soon ceased to be read itself. It died out, as I have said, and is now known only to few of the older members of the community and the profession. It is a book of such a character, that any man at any period of his life might be pardoned the manifestation of some little self-complacency at finding himself the author of it. Many have passed a long life in the profession, and held a high and honorable position in it, without giving any evidence of the mastery of so much of the learning that belongs to it as is contained in this work.

His " Defence of Christianity," written partly before his ordination and published six months afterwards, in August, 1814, was Mr. Everett's legacy to the clerical profession, bequeathed to it before he was invested with a legal manhood. I am aware that their opinions on the Prophets and the Old Testament generally, do not permit some eminent theological scholars to put a very high estimate upon Mr. Everett's " Defence of Christianity," but, for myself, without disparagement of the good he has done, and the honors he has attained in other departments, I cannot but think, that if there be any one event, work, or labor of his varied and useful life, of which he may, on a just estimate of things, be most proud, it is that in the days of his early youth, on the very threshold of his career, he prepared and published this book, which silenced the voice of infidelity and gave peace, satisfaction, and a firm faith to thousands of minds in a young and growing community.

We are not surprised that a career, which began in such industry, in the exhibition of so much learning and such fidelity in improving opportunity, should have gone on to the close increasing in honor and usefulness. I do not propose to follow this career with such minuteness all through, nor would it be proper in me to do so here ; but as I have spoken of the clergyman, I may be permitted to say something of the Professor at Cambridge, as I am the only member of the Society present, who, as a pupil in the Academic Department of the University

had the benefit of his instructions and lectures. Cambridge and the family of President Kirkland having been
my home for several years before I entered college in
1821, not long after he entered upon his professorship,
I knew something about the college, and had ample
opportunity of knowing also the fresh impulse which he
gave to the study of Greek, by the general influence of his
reputation as a Greek scholar, by his occasional presence
at our recitations to the tutors in Greek, by his suggestive
direction or advice to such students as wished to give
special attention to this department, but chiefly by his
lectures on the Greek language and literature, which
were delivered to the senior class, in what was then, there
being three, the second or Spring Term of the college
year. The class graduating in 1825, of which I was a
member, was the last of the six classes who had the
benefit of these lectures. From my recollection of them,
from notes taken at the time, and from the printed synop-
sis which was furnished for our guidance, I have a strong
impression of the extraordinary character of those lectures, as profound, comprehensive, discriminating, and
largely exhaustive of all the learning connected with
their theme. Had he published them when he resigned,
he would have left in his Professor's chair a legacy as
remarkable, in its kind, as his legacy to the pulpit in
his " Defence of Christianity," and secured to himself
such a reputation as a Greek scholar, master of all the
learning appertaining to the history and criticism of
Greek literature, as many a man would have been willing
to rest upon for the remainder of his life.

But while professor at Cambridge, Mr. Everett was interested not simply in his immediate duties, but in whatever touched the welfare and improvement of the college. In all departments his influence was felt, and in one direction he was active in a way which had some connection, I suppose, with his resignation of his professorship to enter upon political life. In 1823, some of the eminent gentlemen at Cambridge, then resident professors, took up the thought, not without some quite substantial reasons, that the "Fellows," as they are termed in the Charter, "Members of the Corporation," as we commonly designate them, should be chosen from among themselves; that the authoritative body controlling the college, having primarily the charge of all its interests, and the conduct of all its affairs, should be composed of the working men on the spot, who best understood its condition and its wants, and were most competent to carry it on successfully, rather than of gentlemen engaged in other occupations, and living in Boston, Salem, or some more distant place. In 1824, they prepared a memorial to this effect, addressed to the Corporation, who referred them to the Board of Overseers, before which body, a hearing, asked for and granted, was subsequently held. The late Andrews Norton, Dexter Professor of Sacred Literature, and Mr. Everett, were selected to represent the memorialists at this hearing. Mr. Norton read a very able paper, marked by the concise accuracy of statement and closeness of reasoning for which he was distinguished. Mr. Everett, without manuscript, with only a few brief memoranda, such as a lawyer

4

would use before a jury, addressed the Board in a
speech occupying more than two hours. He was inter-
rupted at times by gentlemen of the Board adverse to the
position of the memorialists, the accuracy, or pertinence,
or propriety of his statements questioned, and in one
instance, if not more, the decision of the Chair, (Lieut.
Gov. Morton presiding,) that he was " not in order,"
required him to change his line of argument and
remark. Nothing, however, seemed to confuse or discom-
pose him. The situation was novel and trying, yet he
sustained himself with an admirable degree of self-posses-
sion, and conducted his cause with great ability. I have
always supposed that it was the exhibition of his powers
on this occasion, the coolness and tact with which he
conducted himself in an argument, and sometimes almost
a debate, before a body of eminent men, some of whom
were opposed to his position, that first suggested his
nomination to represent Middlesex in Congress, and that
his splendid and eloquent oration before the Phi Beta
Kappa Society, in August, 1824, only helped to confirm
the purpose of his nomination, and secure his election.
Thus much at least is clear, any distrust that may have
been felt in any quarter as to his fitness or competency
for congressional service, in view of his scholastic train-
ing and habits, found a conclusive answer in the manner
in which he bore himself in this hearing before the Board
of Overseers.

But whatever suggested the nomination, it was made,
and he was elected in the autumn of 1824, and, delivering
his lectures for the last time in the spring of 1825, he

resigned and took his seat in Congress in December of
that year. The deep regret felt and expressed by many
at that time, that so much learning, such various abilities,
persuasive eloquence, and rare combination of qualities,
were lost to the direct service of literature and religion,
must be largely diminished, if not entirely extinguished by
his eminent and brilliant success, by his wide spread usefulness in varied departments of public and political life,
by the singular nobleness and purity of his whole career,
and by his constant fidelity and devotedness to the interests
of truth, virtue, and religion. For he seems to me to have
been thus faithful and devoted. I feel disposed to maintain that Mr. Everett was true always to the spirit of his
early vows, and though he did not continue in the administration of religion as an institution of society, he
continued to cultivate its spirit and power in his heart,
and to make it the controlling inspiration and energy of
his life. It is not necessary, nor would it be proper for
me here, to go into an analysis of his speeches, votes,
or conduct at various junctures in our public affairs during
the last forty years, but it seems to me, that whatever
difference of judgment party predilections may dispose us
to entertain about portions of his public career, a broad,
generous, just, and fair review of the whole of it, will lead
every one to concur in the position, that it was all under-
laid and impregnated from the beginning to the end with
a simple, honest, conscientious, patriotic purpose. The
very admirable and beautiful analysis of his character,
which Mr. Hillard has just read before us, seemed to me
to confirm this position, and to give the true explanation

of his course. From his entrance upon public life in
1825, to the spring of 1861, all through those more than
thirty years, in which the struggle between the antago-
nistic elements of liberty and slavery in our government
and institutions came up in various forms, he, in common
with many of our greatest statesmen and large masses of
our people, felt that a certain line of policy was the
wisest and the best, most adapted to keep the peace, to
preserve the Union from dissolution, and the Government
and the country from ruin. Therefore, adhering to this
policy, adopted on conviction, he was for patience, for-
bearance, compromise, concession, for yielding anything
and everything that could, not simply in justice, but in
generosity and honor, be yielded to satisfy those who
were perpetually holding over us the menace of dissolution. Honestly, and in the spirit of a broad patriotism, to
disarm this menace of all occasion and all justification,
was the purpose of his action and policy while in public
office, and of his efforts as a private citizen, and especially
of that grand national pilgrimage which he made with the
life and character of Washington as the theme of a magnificent discourse, which he delivered so many times to such
vast assemblies in all the principal cities of the land, in the
hope that under the shadow of that august name, and by
the glory of a memory so sacred to all of us, he might
allay sectional prejudice and the strife of parties, and
bind all together in a common love and devotion to the
Union. But when this hope failed, and he found that
treason had developed its plans, that rebellion, unfurling its
standard, had inaugurated civil war, then the policy that

had hitherto guided his life was instantly abandoned. He felt that there was no longer any room for concession or compromise, and so gave himself, time, talents, wisdom, strength, all that he had, in all the ways that he could, to support the legitimate Government of the United States, in all the action and policy by which that Government sought to maintain at all hazards and at any cost the integrity of the Union and country which that Government was instituted to preserve. But in all this he was under the inspiration of a patriotism that always dwelt in his heart, though in these latter years he seems to have been raised to an energy, enthusiasm, and earnestness of effort, that indicate a deeper and stronger conviction that he was right than he exhibited or perhaps ever experienced before.

This is the true interpretation, I conceive, to be put upon Mr. Everett's political course as a public man. In our estimate of him intellectually, it will not be maintained, I presume, that Mr. Everett was one of those grand, original, creative, inventive, productive minds, that strike out new paths in science, philosophy, or the policies of States. Such minds come upon the world only in the cycle of centuries. But he had a mind of vast powers, capable of comprehending principles, gathering up details, and making use of both. He had a conscientious, unwearied industry, and consequently accumulated vast stores of knowledge in all the departments of art, science, history, and literature. He had a wonderful memory, raised to its highest power by constant culture and exercise. He had a rare combination of intellectual, moral, and physical faculties, and above all, he had the power of using all his faculties and all his acquisitions with grace, beauty, and dignity, so that he touched nothing that he did not illustrate and adorn, and came before us ever, on all occasions, with a freshness and force that charmed and instructed. As is well known to his intimate friends, he was singularly kind, tender, faithful and true in every domestic relation of life, and to all the claims of kindred and friendship, with a warm heart under a reserved manner, and a sympathizing spirit under lips often reticent ; and if, remembering this, we do justice to his private, personal character, and then look at his public career, at the wide circle of varied offices which he successively held, at the labor performed, the ability displayed in each ; if we add to these his works as a scholar and a literary man, — his magnificent orations, all of them such masterpieces of eloquence, pure and elevating in their impression ; broad, noble, generous in their thoughts ; breathing ever the spirit of piety and patriotism, fitted to instruct our people and unfold our history, while they adorn our literature, — his numerous contributions to the periodical press, especially those to the *North American Review*, often profound discussions of grave questions in literature and philosophy ; if we then crown all with the noble and patriotic labors of the last four years, we find enough surely in this survey to win for him alike our admiration and our gratitude ; enough, and more than enough, to dispose us to bow before his memory in reverence, and accord to him the name and the fame of being a

great man. Where shall we find one who in such varied
spheres has done so much and done it so well? His
was a noble life and character, and his career, followed
from the beginning to the end, was marvellous in its
early precocity, its growing wisdom, its ever increasing
breadth, and its grand conclusion. He was a Franklin
Medal scholar in the old North Grammar School at the
age of ten, a Franklin Medal scholar at the Public Latin
School at thirteen, chief in his class at Cambridge at
seventeen, a tutor in the University at eighteen, an
ordained minister of the Gospel before he was twenty,
appointed to a professorship of Greek literature before he
was twenty-one, elected a member of Congress at thirty;
and thence, after a few years' service in the halls of national legislation, he was called to the Chief Magistracy
of this State, all of whose affairs he directed with wisdom,
dignity, and usefulness, — and thence to represent his
country abroad in one of its most important and honorable
foreign embassies, — and thence, on his return to his
native land, to preside over the interests of learning at its
oldest and most advanced University, — and thence to a
seat in the National Cabinet for the Department of State,
— and thence to a seat in that august body, the Senate of
the United States, — and thence, through noble and patriotic labors, to a higher and broader place than he had
ever held before, in the hearts of his countrymen; and
when he had attained to this grand preëminence, to be
the foremost private citizen in all the land, holding no
public office, but wielding a power and doing a service
which mere office could never do, wearing this great

distinction with unaffected modesty, walking among us
with none of the infirmities but all the glory of age upon
his person, and the wisdom of age in his speech, — then
the beautiful and fitting end came, and without a linger-
ing sickness, without a shadow upon his noble faculties,
suddenly he died. Alone in his solitary preëminence,
alone, as it were, he died; and that cold Sunday morning
air, that brought a chill to our bodies, as it swept through
our streets and by our doors with its sad announcement,
" Edward Everett is dead! " brought a chill to our hearts
which the warmth of many summers will not dispel, and
left an image and a memory there that will abide with all
of us, beautiful and bright, so long as we live. Mr.
President, I second the resolutions.

The Hon. John C. Gray then spoke as follows : —

MR. PRESIDENT: Apart from the intimation with
which I have been honored through you and other
respected friends, I might have been prompted by my
own feelings to offer a few remarks on this most solemn
and interesting occasion. One of the few remaining
companions of my youth has departed. An uninterrupted
friendship of nearly sixty years has been dissolved.
But I am not here to speak of my own loss or my own
feelings, but to contribute in doing justice to the memory
of the deceased. The theme is a most copious one.
It is not my purpose to analyze the character of our
friend, still less to indulge in vague and extravagant
eulogy. I prefer to speak briefly of those points in his
character which have stamped themselves most deeply

on my own memory. We were of the same class in college, and for two years of our college life occupied the same apartment. I have ever looked back on that association as one of the most valuable, as well as one of the most gratifying, of my early days. His ripeness of judgment was not less remarkable than the precocity of his genius. But there is yet higher praise.

I can say, and you perceive that I had some means of knowing, that I never knew one who preserved a more unruffled temper. Not a single instance can I recollect of irritability. Such a temper must of necessity be its own reward, and I think we may fairly ascribe to it much of his subsequent greatness. For, sir, among the many weighty truths which fell from his lips, I recollect none more striking than a remark in his lecture to the working-men, while recommending the improvement of their leisure hours. " Generally speaking," he observes, " our business allows us time enough, if our passions would but spare us." Never man more faithfully practised as he preached. In the course of his life he had his share of those chastening dispensations which come in various shapes and degrees to every one. But none of them caused the slightest remission in his unwearied industry. The great summons which awaits us all found him at his work, and so it would have done, come when it might. I shall say little more of his college life. New England education was not then what it has since become. Mr. Everett improved his literary advantages to the utmost, and bore off the first honors.

I pass over his short but brilliant ministry in the pulpit and his years of assiduous study in foreign countries. Shortly after his return he assumed the post of editor of our leading review. It was at a most interesting period. This country and Great Britain had closed their contests by an honorable peace, and there was on our side a general disposition to cultivate a friendly and respectful feeling towards our late adversaries. This certainly was not fully reciprocated. The leading British reviews seemed to agree in nothing so much as in speaking of our country and its institutions with hatred or contempt. Mr. Everett felt it his duty to stand forth in defence of our good name. It is not a little to his praise that while he did this most ably and earnestly, he always preserved the dignity befitting his cause and himself, and never descended to meet his antagonists with their own weapons. There is good reason to believe that his candid and manly appeals to the good sense of the people of England were not in vain, and that they contributed to create among educated Englishmen a feeling better becoming them and more just to us, a feeling which for a long time seemed prevalent, and which we had hoped would have been general and permanent. Mr. Everett's able and eloquent defences of the good name of his country naturally led to invitations to serve her in public trusts.

I will not pretend to say that such invitations were unacceptable. Suffice it to remark that, if he desired public life, he never accepted an office which was not properly offered, never purchased one by pledges in advance, direct or indirect, and never for a moment used his position for the emolument of himself or his friends. What I have more to say will be devoted to his personal character. A spotless private character has ever been considered in New England, and I trust not in New England alone, as one of the elements of true greatness, and Heaven forbid that it should ever be held in light estimation! This merit was his beyond impeachment, — not his alone, most certainly, but his eminence in other respects rendered his example in this more conspicuous, and thus more widely beneficial. Of this character I shall notice one leading feature, — I mean his wakeful and unremitted disposition to benefit others. If judged by his fruits, we must allow that Edward Everett was a most benevolent man. His exertions and resources of mind, body, or estate were most freely imparted on every reasonable call, — I should say on every reasonable opportunity. Whether the applicant was a friend or a stranger, the occasion conspicuous or unconspicuous, it was enough for him that he could serve or oblige in great or small. And now, sir, I will close by a few inquiries. No one will suspect me of disparaging any of our eminent men, departed or surviving, when I ask —

Has any one among us ever been more distinguished by a noble use of noble endowment? Has there been any one less obnoxious to the charge of talents wasted and time misspent; any one who could say with more truth in words he once felt compelled to utter, that he knew not how the bread of idleness tasted? Has any one done more, by his wise and eloquent productions, to elevate, instruct, and refine the minds of his countrymen? Finally, has any one been more distinguished by exemplary fidelity in public office and by constant kindness and benevolence in private life? Few higher eulogies can be uttered than the reply which must rise to the lips of every one.

George Ticknor, Esq. then addressed the meeting as follows:—

MR. PRESIDENT: I ask your permission to say a few words concerning the eminent associate and cherished friend whom we have lost,— so sadly, so suddenly lost. It is but little that I can say becoming the occasion, so well was he known of all; for, in his early youth, he rose to a height, which has led us to watch and honor and understand, from the first, his long and brilliant career.

On looking back over the two centuries and a half of this our New England history, I recollect not more than three or four persons who, during as many years of a life protracted as his was beyond threescore and ten, have so much occupied the attention of the country,— I do not remember a single one, who has presented himself under such various, distinct, and remarkable aspects to classes of our community so separate, thus commanding a degree of interest from each, whether scholars, theologians, or statesmen, which in the aggregate of its popular influence has become so extraordinary. For he has been, to a marvellous degree successful, in whatever he has touched. His whole way of life for above fifty years can now be traced back by the monuments which he

erected with his own hand as he advanced; each seeming, at the time, to be sufficient for the reputation of one
man. Few here are old enough to remember when the
first of these graceful monuments rose before us; none
of us I apprehend is so young, that he will survive the
splendor of their long line. And, now that we have
come to its end, and that it seems as if the whole air
were filled with our sorrowful and proud recollections, as
it is with the light at noonday, we feel with renewed
force that we have known him as we have known very
few men of our time. And this is true. How, then,
can I say anything that shall be worthy of memory;
still less anything that is fit for record?

When he was ten or eleven years of age and I was
about three years older, his family came to live within a
few doors of my father's house and subsequently removed
to a contiguous estate. But, at this time, Mr. President,
when the City of Boston, I suppose, was not one fifth as
large as it is now, neighborhood implied kindly acquaintance. I soon knew his elder brother, Alexander, then
the leader of his class at Cambridge, while I was a
student in a class one year later, at Dartmouth College.
I at once conceived a strong admiration for that remarkable scholar;—an admiration, let me add, which has never
been diminished since. The younger brother, of whom
I saw little, was then in that humble school in Short
Street which he has made classical by his occasional
allusions to it, and to the two Websters who were his
teachers there. From the elder of these, who was frequently at my father's house, I used to hear much about

the extraordinary talents and progress of this younger Everett; praise which my admiration of his brother prevented me, I fear, from receiving, for a time, with so glad a welcome as I ought to have done. During the two or three subsequent years, while the younger brother was at Exeter or beginning his career at Cambridge, I knew little of him, though I was much with the elder and belonged to at least one pleasant club of which he was a member.

The first occasion on which the younger scholar's delightful character broke upon me, with its true attributes, is still fresh in my recollection. It was in the summer of 1809. Mr. Alexander Everett was then about to embark for St. Petersburg, as the private secretary of Mr. John Quincy Adams, and a few nights before he left us, he gave a supper—saddened, indeed, by the parting that was so soon to follow, but still a most agreeable supper—to eight or ten of his personal friends, one of whom (Dr. Bigelow) I now see before me;—the last, except myself, remaining of that well remembered symposium. The younger brother was there, so full of gayety—unassuming but irrepressible—so full of whatever is attractive in manner or in conversation, that I was perfectly carried captive by his light and graceful humor. And this, let me here say, has always been a true element of his character. He was never at any period of his life a saturnine man. In his youth he overflowed with animal spirits; and, although from the time of his entrance into political life, with the grave cares and duties that were imposed upon him, the lightheartedness of his nature was somewhat oppressed or obscured, it was always there. There was never a time I think — excepting in those days of trial and sorrow that come to all — in which, among the private friends with whom he was most intimate, he was not cheerful, nay charmingly amusing. It was so the very day before his death. He was suffering from an oppression on the lungs; and, as I sat with him, he could speak only in whispers; but, even then, his natural playfulness was not wanting.

But from the time of that delightful supper in 1809, my regard never failed to be fastened on him. At first, during his under-graduate's life, at Cambridge, I saw him seldom. But in that simpler stage of our society, when the interests of men were so different from what they have become since, all who concerned themselves about letters, were familiar with what was done and doing in Cambridge. Everett, youthful as he was, was eminently the first scholar there, and we all knew it. We all — or, at least, all of us who were young — read the " Harvard Lyceum," which he edited, and which, I may almost say, he filled with his scholarship and humor.

In 1811 he was graduated with the highest honors, and pronounced, with extraordinary grace of manner, a short oration, on — if I rightly remember — " The Difficulties attending a Life of Letters," which delighted a crowded audience, attracted more than was usual by the expectations that waited on what is called " The first part." But thus far, what was most known of his life was strictly academic, and was only more widely spread than an academic reputation is wont to be because he was himself already so full of recognized promise and power. His time, in fact, was not yet come. But the next year it came. He was invited to deliver the customary poem at Commencement, before the "Phi Beta Kappa Society." It was not, perhaps, a period, when much success could have been anticipated for anybody, on a merely literary occasion. The war with England had been declared only a few weeks earlier and men felt gloomy and disheartened at the prospect before them. Still more recently Buckminster had died, only twenty-eight years old, but loved and admired, as few men ever have been in this community; — mourned, too, as a loss to the beginnings of true scholarship among us, which many a scholar then thought might hardly be repaired. But, as in all cases of a general stir in the popular feeling, there was an excitement abroad which permitted the minds of men to be turned and wielded in directions widely different from that of the prevailing current. The difficulty was to satisfy the demands in such a disturbed condition of things.

Mr. Everett was then just in that "opening manhood" which Homer, with his unerring truth, has called "the fairest term of life." And how handsome he was, Mr. President! We all know how remarkable was Milton's early beauty. An engraving of him — a fine one — by Vertue, from a portrait preserved in the Onslow family, and painted when the poet was about twenty, is well known. But, sir, so striking was the resemblance of this engraving to our young friend, that I remember often seeing a copy of it inscribed with his name in capital letters, and am unable to say that the inscription was amiss. Radiant, then, with such personal attractions, he rose before an audience already disposed to receive him with extraordinary kindness.

His subject was, " American Poets," ·certainly not a very promising one. Of course his treatment of it was essentially didactic; but there was such a mixture of good-natured satire in it, so much more praise willingly accorded than was really deserved, such humorous and happy allusions to what was local, personal, and familiar to all, and such solemn and tender passages about the condition of our society, and its anxieties and losses,— that it was received with an applause which, in some respects, I have never known equalled. Graver and grander success I have often known to be achieved, on greater occasions, not only by others but by himself. But never did I witness such clear, unmingled delight. Everything was forgotten but the speaker and what he chose we should remember.

This success, it should be recollected, was gained when Mr. Everett was only a little more than eighteen years old. But, sir, in fact, it had been gained earlier. The poem had been read when he was only about seventeen, before a club of college friends in the latter part of his senior year, and had now been fitted by a few additions, for its final destination. Its publication was immediately demanded and urged. But on the whole it was determined not to give it fully to the world. Four copies, however, were privately struck off on large paper, one of which I received at the time from the author, and thirty-

six more in common octavo, which were at once dis-
tributed to other eager friends. But this was by no means
enough. A little later, therefore, there were printed,
with slight alterations, sixty copies more, of which he
gave me two, in an extra form, marked with his fair
autograph. I know not where three others are now to
be found; though I trust, from the great contemporary
interest in the poem itself, and from its real value, that
many copies of it have been saved.

It is written in the versification consecrated by the
success of Dryden and Pope; and if it contains lines
marked by the characteristics of the early age at which it
was produced, there is yet a power in it, a richness of
thought, and a graceful finish, of which probably few men
at thirty would have been found capable. At any rate, in
the hundred and more years during which verse had then
been printed in these Colonies and States, not two hundred
pages, I think, can now be found, which can be read
with equal interest and pleasure.

It was only a few weeks afterwards, as nearly as I
recollect, that he began to preach. I heard his first two
sermons, delivered to a small congregation in a neighbor-
ing town, and I heard him often afterwards. The effect
was always the same. There was not only the attractive
manner, which we had already witnessed and admired,
but there was, besides, a devout tenderness, which had
hardly been foreseen. The main result, however, had
been anticipated. He was, in a few months, settled over
the church in Brattle Street, with the assent and admiration of all.

But, in the midst of his success in the pulpit, he was turned aside to become a controversial theologian. Early in the autumn of 1813, Mr. George B. English published a small book, entitled, "The Grounds of Christianity Examined by Comparing the New Testament with the Old." It was, in fact, an attack on the truth of the Christian religion, in the sense of Judaism. Its author, whom I knew personally, was a young man of very pleasant intercourse, and a great lover of books, of which he had read many, but with little order or well-defined purpose. He would, I think, have been a man of letters, if such a path had been open to him. A profession, however, was needful. He studied law, but became 'dissatisfied with it. He studied divinity, but was never easy in his course. His mind was never well balanced, or well settled upon anything. He was always an adventurer — just as much so in the scholarlike period of his life, as he was afterwards, when he served under Ismail Pasha, in Egypt, and attempted to revive the ancient war-chariots armed with scythes.

His ill-constructed book received several answers, direct and indirect, from the pulpit and the press; but none of them was entirely satisfactory, because their authors had not frequented the strange by-paths of learning in which Mr. English had for some time been wandering with perverse preference. Mr. Everett, however, followed him everywhere with a careful scholarship and exact logic unknown to his presumptuous adversary. His "Defence of Christianity" was published in 1814, and I still possess one, out of half a dozen copies of it that were

printed for the author's friends, on extra paper, and are
become curious as showing how ill understood, in those
simpler days, were the dainty luxuries of bibliography.
But the proper end of the book was quickly attained.
Mr. English's imperfect and unsound learning was demol-
ished at a blow; and, as has just been so happily said by
Dr. Lothrop, the whole controversy, even Mr. Everett's
part of it, is forgotten, because it has been impossible
to keep up any considerable interest in a question which
he had so absolutely settled.   Mr. Everett's "Defence,"
however, will always remain a remarkable book.   Some
years after its publication, Professor Monk, of Cambridge,
the biographer of Bentley, and himself afterwards Bishop
of Gloucester, told me that he did not think any Episcopal
library in England could be accounted complete which
did not possess a copy of it.

In the winter following the publication of this book —
that is, in the winter of 1814–15 — he was elected Professor of Greek Literature.   I was then at the South,
having made up my mind to pass some time at the University of Göttingen, and was endeavoring, chiefly among
the Germans in the interior of Pennsylvania, to obtain
information concerning the modes of teaching in Germany, about which there then prevailed in New England
an absolute ignorance now hardly to be conceived.   With
equal surprise and delight, I received letters from my
friend telling me of his appointment, and that, to qualify
himself for the place offered him, he should endeavor to
go with me upon what we both regarded as a sort of
adventure, to Germany.   Perhaps I should add that this

sudden change in his course of life excited no small com-
ment at the time, and that, especially by a part of the
parish whose brilliant anticipations he thus disappointed,
it was not accepted in a kindly spirit. But of its wisdom
and rightfulness there was soon no doubt in the mind of
anybody.

We embarked in April, 1815, and passed a few weeks
in London, during the exciting period of Bonaparte's last
campaign, and just at the time of the battle of Waterloo.
But we were in a hurry to be at work. We hastened,
therefore, through Holland, stopping chiefly to buy books,
and early in August were already in the chosen place of
our destination. It was our purpose to remain there a
year. But the facilities for study were such as we had
never heard or dreamt of. My own residence was in
consequence protracted to a year and nine months, and
Mr. Everett's was protracted yet six months longer —
both of us leaving the tempting school at last sorry and
unsatisfied.

How well he employed his time there the great results
shown in his whole subsequent life have enabled the
world to judge. I witnessed the process from day to day.
We were constantly together. Except for the first few
months, when we could not make convenient arrange-
ments for it, we lived in contiguous rooms in the same
house — the house of Bouterwek, the literary historian,
and a favorite teacher in the university. During the
vacations — except one, when he went to the Hague, to
see his brother Alexander, then our Secretary of Legation
in Holland — we travelled together about Germany; and

every day in term time we went more or less to the same
private teachers, and the same lecturers. But he struck
in his studies much more widely than I did. To say
nothing of his constant, indefatigable labor upon the
Greek with Dissen, he occupied himself a good deal with
Arabic under Eichhorn, he attended lectures upon modern
history by Heeren, and upon the civil law by Hugo, and
he followed besides the courses of other professors, whose
teachings I did not frequent and whose names I no longer
remember.

His power of labor was prodigious; unequalled in my
experience. One instance of it — the more striking, perhaps, because disconnected from his regular studies — is,
I think, worth especial notice. We had been in Göttingen, I believe, above a year, and he was desirous to send
home something of what he had learnt about the modes
of teaching, not only there but in our visits to the univer-
sities of Leipzig, Halle, Jena, and Berlin, and to the great
preparatory schools of Meissen, and Pforte. He had, as
nearly as I can recollect, just begun this task. But how
so voluminous a matter was to be sent home was an
important question. Regular packets there were none,
even between New York and Liverpool. We depended,
therefore, very much on accident — altogether on tran-
sient vessels. Opportunities from Hamburg were rare
and greatly valued. Just at this time our kind mer-
cantile correspondents at that port gave us sudden notice
that a vessel for Boston would sail immediately. There
was not a moment to be lost; Mr. Everett threw everything else aside, and worked for thirty-five consecutive

hours on his letter, despatching it as the mail was closing.
But, though sadly exhausted by his labor, he was really
uninjured, and in a day or two was fully refreshed and
restored. I need not say that a man who did this was in
earnest in what he undertook. But let me add, Mr.
President, that, by the constant, daily exercise of dispo-
sitions and powers like these, he laid during those two or
three years in Göttingen, the real foundations on which
his great subsequent success, in so many widely different
ways, safely rested. I feel as sure of this as I do of any
fact of the sort within my knowledge.

When I left Göttingen, he and a young American
friend (Stephen H. Perkins)—then under his charge, and
who still survives—accompanied me on my first day's
journey. At Hesse Cassel we separated, thinking to
meet again in the south of Europe, and visit together
Greece and Asia Minor, which, from the time of the
appearance of "Childe Harold," four or five years earlier,
had been much in our young thoughts and imaginations.
But "Forth rushed the Levant and the Ponent winds."
A few months afterwards, at Paris, I received the appointment of Professor of French and Spanish Literature, at
Cambridge; and, from that moment, it was as plain that
my destination was Madrid, as it was that he was bound
to go to Athens and Constantinople. We did not, therefore, meet again until his return home, in the autumn of
1819, where I had preceded him by a few months.

From this time Mr. Everett's life has been almost constantly a public one, and all have been able to judge him
freely and fully. He began his lectures on Greek litera-

ture at Cambridge the next summer, and I went from
Boston regularly to hear them, for the pleasure and
instruction they gave me. The notes I then took of them,
and which I still preserve, will bear witness to the merit
just ascribed to them by the friend on my left, who heard
the same course somewhat later.

But Mr. Everett was, in another sense, already a public
man. From the natural concern he felt in the fate of a
country he had so recently visited, he took a great interest,
as early as 1821–23, in the Greek Revolution, and wrote
and spoke on it, both as a philanthropic and as a political
question. In 1824 he was elected to Congress. There
and elsewhere, like other public men of eminence, he has
had his political trials and his political opponents ; sometimes generous, sometimes unworthy, but never touching the unspotted purity of his character and purposes.
All such discussions, however, find no becoming place
within these doors. We recognize here no such divisions
of opinion respecting our lamented associate. We remember his great talents, and the gentleness that added to
their power ; his extraordinary scholarship, and the rich
fruits it bore ; his manifold public services, and the just
honors that have followed them. All this we remember.
In all of it we rejoice. We recollect, too, that for five-and-
forty years, he has been our pride and ornament, as a
member of this Society. But we recognize no external
disturbing element in these our happy recollections. To
us, he has always been the same. At any meeting that
we have held since he became fully known to us and to
the country, the beautiful, appropriate, and truthful reso-

lutions now on your table, might — if he had just been taken from us as he has been now — have been passed by us with as much earnestness and unanimity, as they will be amidst our sorrow to-night. They do but fitly complete our record of what has always been true. And let us feel thankful, as we adopt this record and make it our own, that — grand and gratifying as it is — neither the next generation nor any that may follow will desire to have a word of it obliterated or altered.

Hon. John H. Clifford then proceeded as follows :—

Mr. President : Having been unable to participate in the last offices of respect to the remains of our departed associate, and feeling obliged to decline the distinguished service to which I was invited, of pronouncing a more elaborate address upon his life and character before the two Houses of the Legislature, I could not forego the opportunity of uniting in this office of commemoration, with an Association in which he took so generous an interest, and of which he was so eminent a member.

However inadequate must be any expression of my sense of the loss we have sustained, I cannot doubt that the assurance of a simple, heartfelt tribute of personal affection and gratitude, when he was to be remembered in a circle like this, would have been more grateful to *him* than any studied words of eulogy, though they were polished into a rhetoric as brilliant as his own.

It is thus only, that I desire to speak of him — my honored chief, my wise and trusted counsellor — my ever constant friend. It was from his hands that I received,

now just thirty years ago, my first commission in the
service of the State; and from that period up to the
close of the last month of the last year, he honored
me with a correspondence which I have carefully preserved as a precious possession for myself and for my
children. You will pardon me, Mr. President, if, in
this brief review of what I owe to the influence of his
friendship and his counsels, I shall invoke his presence,
still to speak to us, by a free and unreserved reference
to this correspondence.

Admitted to the intimate intercourse of a member of his
military family, during the entire term of his service as
Governor of the Commonwealth, he never afterwards
ceased to manifest the interest in me which that intercourse implied, and the value of which no poor words
of mine, of public or of private acknowledgment can
ever measure or repay. Of that military family, Mr.
President,— and " we were seven,"— who bore his commission during those four years of brilliant service to his
native Commonwealth, you and I are the only survivors,
to render these last honors to our illustrious chief.

In the review of his remarkable career, to which,
since its triumphant close on earth, the minds of so
many have been turned who never knew him otherwise
than in his public character, I am persuaded that some
impressions respecting him, which those who were
brought nearest to him know to be utterly unfounded,
are certain to be corrected when the materials of a just
judgment of all that he was, and all that he did, are
open to the examination of his countrymen.

It has been said of him that he was of a cold and
unsympathizing nature. There never was a more mistaken judgment of any public man than this. If
he possessed any trait more distinctly marked than
another, it was his unfaltering fidelity to his friends,
and his warm and generous interest in everything that
touched their happiness and welfare, as well in the
trials and the sorrows, as in the successes and the sun-
shine of life.

While he was representing the country with such
signal ability at the Court of St. James, and in the
midst of the grave and perplexing questions which he
there discussed and disposed of with such masterly
skill, I had occasion to communicate to him the death
of a much loved child, in whom he had taken great
interest, and who bore his name. In a letter written
on the receipt of the intelligence, and under circumstances that might well have excused him from an
immediate reply,— and which would have excused him,
if that reply had been prompted by anything less than
a sincere and unaffected sympathy, which does not
belong to a cold and formal nature,— he says: " I was
staying at Sir Robert Peel's, with a very agreeable
party, consisting of several of the cabinet ministers, and
my diplomatic brethren, when I received your letter,
which has cast a shade of sadness over my visit that
I feel as little inclination as ability to throw off. . .
. . . But let us not speak of our beloved ones as
taken from us. They are, in truth, not lost, but gone
before. They have accomplished, in the dawn of life

the work which grows harder, the longer the time that
is given us to do it."

Equally erroneous, in my judgment, is the opinion that
Mr. Everett, as a public man, was lacking in moral
courage. There were occasions in his life when it would
have required less courage, and have cost a smaller sacri-
fice to escape this imputation, and secure to himself the
popular favor, than it did to invite it. But his resolute
adherence to his own conscientious convictions, his large
and comprehensive patriotism, his unswerving nationality
and love of the Union, and the knowledge which a scholar's studies and a statesman's observations had given him
of the perils by which that Union was environed, closed
many an avenue of popularity to him, which bolder, but
not more courageous, public men than he could consent
to walk in.

If timidity consists in an absence of all temerity and
rashness, of entire freedom from that reckless spirit which
so often leads "fools to rush in where angels fear to
tread," let it be ever remembered to his honor, that Mr.
Everett was a timid statesman. But if the virtue of
moderation is still to be counted among the excellent
qualities of a ruler or counsellor, in conducting the com-
plex and delicate questions of policy which affect the
well-being of a country like ours, and which bear upon its
future fortunes as well as its present favor, let it also be
remembered that our departed statesman, while he ad-
hered inflexibly to his convictions of the right, was not
" ashamed to let his moderation be known unto all men."

In this aspect of his character, it has seemed to me that

the great *Pater Patriæ*, whom he had so diligently studied, and his oration upon whom wrought as great a work upon his countrymen as his unsurpassed biographical sketch of him in the " Encyclopædia Britannica" has had upon the foreign estimate of Washington, was " his great example, as he was his theme."

It has been not an unfrequent criticism upon Mr. Everett's career, that it was in a certain sense a failure, because, with his scholarly tastes, his patient industry, his affluent learning and his great opportunities, he would leave behind him no " great work" as the fruit of all his accomplishments and powers. If it be a worthy ambition in one of great endowments and liberal culture, to do the greatest good to the greatest number of his fellow-men, and to make the world better for his having lived in it, this is a mistaken criticism. It is true his resources were ample to have accomplished any " great work," such as this criticism implies, in any of the fields of intellectual activity, from which great scholars gather their ripened harvests. He could have graced the shelves of our libraries with precious octavos of history, or science, or literature. But to have done this he would have foregone that " greater work" which he did accomplish, and of which the three volumes already published, to be followed we trust by many more, will stand forever as the witness and the memorial — " *Non omnia possumus omnes.*" And he appointed to himself the nobler task of elevating the public taste, — of bringing before a working people the highest truths of philosophy in a style of adaptation to their wants before unknown — of diffusing throughout the com-

munity a knowledge of great historical events and their
application to the duties of living men, — of implanting in
the breasts of the people a reverence for their God-fearing
ancestors, and in justifying the ways of Providence to
them and their posterity, — of displaying before them the
brightest deeds and the most heroic sacrifices of patriotism, and thereby inspiring in them the warmest love of
their country, and instructing them in the duties they
owed to her, — all these, and more, of the glorious proofs
that his life was a noble success and in no sense a failure,
glow in every page of his writings, not one of which in
dying would he need to blot, from that first lecture
before the Mechanics' Institute in Charlestown, down to
that last fervid, Christian appeal in Faneuil Hall.

Mr. President, I speak in the faith of the clearest conviction, that whatever of unjust, or censorious, or honestly
mistaken judgment, has ever been passed upon our departed friend, will be surely modified, if not entirely
reversed, in all candid minds, under the lights with which
a true and complete history of his life will illuminate it,
from its earliest promise to its latest most glorious record.
Already one of his contemporaries, who has made his
own name " imperishable in immortal song," in words of
manly confession, as honorable to their author as they are
just to the memory of him of whom they were spoken,
has anticipated the verdict of history.

" If," says Mr. Bryant, " I have uttered anything in
derogation of Mr. Everett's public character at times when
it seemed to me that he did not resist with becoming
spirit the aggressions of wrong, I now, looking back upon

his noble record of the last four years, retract it at his
grave, — I lay upon his hearse the declaration of my
sorrow that I saw not then the depth of his worth, — that
I did not discern under the conservatism that formed a
part of his nature, that generous courage which a great
emergency could so nobly awaken."

But the praises of men were now of little worth, had
we not one source of pride and affection open to us in the
contemplation of this beneficent life, the value of which
no words of eulogy, apt as they are to run into exaggera-
tion, can express too strongly. The manifold temptations
of public life, whether insinuating themselves through
our domestic politics, or the social and political ethics of
the national capitol, in the arts of diplomacy or through
the enervating allurements of foreign courts, which in
some of their Protean forms are so apt to assail the home-
taught virtue of our public men, never left a trace of their
influence upon the purity of his unsullied character. To
those who had the closest view of him, there was always
apparent his constant recognition of the presence and
direction of a Higher Power in all the concerns of life.
Abundant illustrations of this, indeed, may be found in his
published works. Who that has read it, who especially
that had your privilege and mine, Mr. President, of listening to it as it fell from his lips, can have forgotten that
magnificent passage, in my judgment the most eloquent
he ever uttered, in his speech at the centennial celebration
at Barnstable in 1839? — a passage which the late Chief
Justice Shaw, who was present, declared to me was, in his
opinion, unsurpassed in modern history.

After describing the condition of "the Mayflower
freighted with the destinies of a continent, as she crept
almost sinking into Provincetown harbor, utterly inca-
pable of living through another gale, approaching the
shore precisely where the broad sweep of this remarkable
headland presents almost the only point at which for
hundreds of miles she could with any ease have made a
harbor," he adds: "I feel my spirit raised above the
sphere of mere natural agencies. I see the mountains of
New England rising from their rocky thrones. They rush
forward into the ocean, settling down as they advance;
and there they range themselves, a mighty bulwark
around the heaven-directed vessel. Yes, the everlasting
God himself stretches out the arm of his mercy and his
power in substantial manifestations, and gathers the meek
company of his worshippers as in the hollow of his
hand."

But a more striking, because a more spontaneous
expression of the same characteristic spirit, is contained
in a letter of farewell which I received from him, dated at
New York on the day before his embarkation for Europe
with his whole family in the summer of 1840, and of
course written amidst all the distractions incident to the
preparations for his voyage.

The intelligence of the burning of the packet ship
Poland at sea, and the rescue of her passengers from
imminent peril by a passing vessel, had then just been
received in this country. "The fate of the Poland," he
writes, "makes me feel strongly how near to death we
are in the midst of life. I embark with all my treasures

with some misgivings. But having undertaken the voyage from proper motives, I seem to be in the path of duty, and I am sure I am in the hand of God. There are many paths to his presence. And whether they lead us singly, or in families, or companies, — whether by a bed of languishing on land, or the blazing deck of a burning vessel, or the dark abyss of the sea, can be of but little consequence in the existence of an undying spirit."

When his own hour had come, Mr. President, it was through no such avenue of suspense and sufferings as these that his Heavenly Father took him to himself. But in welcoming him, as our faith assures us, to the rewards of a " good and faithful servant," He bore him from our sight so graciously as to leave us nothing to regret from him, either in his death or in his life. Why should we mourn over such a death, — the serene close of such a life on earth, the entrance upon the assured rewards of the Life Eternal?

> " If ever lot was prosperously cast,
> If ever life was like the lengthened flow
> Of some sweet music, sweetness to the last,
> 'T was his." . . . .

Not the music of that matchless voice alone, whose inspiring cadences seem still to linger in our ears, as we assemble in this room, where it so often charmed and instructed us, but the diviner harmony to which he gave such magnificent expression by a rounded and completed life, — a life that was mercifully spared to his country for its greatest work during its closing years; whose music, during those years of a nation's regeneration, was but a prolongation of the music of the Union, by which he marched, himself, and inspired his countrymen to march, to the great conflict with treason and with wrong.

Here, and wherever throughout the world, in all coming time, the gospel of constitutional liberty is preached among men, shall this, his last, greatest work, " be told as a memorial of him." One word more, Mr. President, and my grateful task is done.

In the correspondence from which I have so freely quoted, I found, a day or two ago, a striking passage, which seems to me a fitting close for this feeble tribute to the memory of a loved and honored friend. In a letter written to me from Washington early in 1854, the year that he resigned his place in the Senate of the United States, he says: "I have never filled an office which I did not quit more cheerfully than I entered. I am not sure that it is not so in most cases with the last great act of retirement, not from the offices and duties of life, but from life itself."

Brethren, to what far-off sphere of celestial fruition may we not, without presumption, in that spirit of faith which he so strongly cherished, follow our departed associate, and hear again the music of that voice, repeating this sentiment, now verified and made certain in the supreme experience of that last Sabbath morning?

Dr. Walker spoke as follows : —

Mr. PRESIDENT: Leaving it for others to speak of Mr. Everett's eminence as a scholar and as a statesman, and of the purity and beauty of his daily life, I ask permission to say a few words of his administration as President of Harvard College. There is, I believe, a prevailing impression in the community, that this part of his public career was less successful than the rest. If so, it is to be imputed, in no small measure, to three ·causes which have hindered his merits and services as Head of the University from being duly appreciated.

The first of these causes was his known distaste for the office. Most of us remember, that when he was appointed to the place, the community were of one mind as to his being precisely the man to fill it, — with a single exception; but that was an important exception, for it was *himself.* This distaste was never entirely overcome; and there are those who have construed it into evidence of want of success. They might have done so with some show of reason, if it had grown up in the office; for, in that case, it might be regarded as resulting, at least in some degree, from disappointed hopes. But when it is considered that the distaste was as strong, and perhaps stronger, when he accepted the office, than when he laid it down, there would seem to be no ground for such a construction.

The second cause which has hindered the public from duly appreciating Mr. Everett's services to the College as President, is found in the nature of the reforms and improvements attempted and actually introduced by him. With his accustomed method and thoroughness, he could not do otherwise than begin at the beginning. Accordingly, one of his first undertakings was to prepare and

publish, under the proper authorities, a careful revision
of the college laws. This was a most important and
necessary work, which cost months of anxious labor; yet
not likely to attract public attention, nor even to be known
beyond the precincts of the University. Again, he believed that all improvements in the college, to be of much
solidity, must have their foundation in its improved moral
and religious condition. No president ever labored more
assiduously or more anxiously for this end, nor, considering the time occupied, with more success. Indeed, I
cannot help thinking that it is for the measures he instituted or suggested with a view to promote the moral
elevation of the college, that its friends have most reason
to hold him in grateful remembrance. Yet these also
were matters which, from their very nature, did not admit
of display, and some of them not even of publicity; nay
more, in the beginning they were not unlikely to occasion
some degree of opposition and trouble.

But the principal cause hindering a due appreciation of
Mr. Everett's presidency of the college, brief as it was, is
doubtless this very brevity. If his health had permitted
him to retain the office ten years, I have no doubt that
many things which were offensive to him would have
disappeared. His attention, meanwhile, would have been
turned to proper academical reforms, noticeable in themselves, and bringing the college into notice by extending
its influence and fame. And this, together with the just
pride taken in his distinguished name, and the unsurpassed dignity with which he represented the University
on all public occasions, would have made his administra-

tion forever illustrious in the annals of the college; and even, within its limited scope, as illustrious *for him* as any other part of his public career. Nor is this all. It would then have been seen that the first four years, those which we really had, were an appropriate and necessary introduction to the whole; and as such, *they* would have come in for their full share of the glory.

Dr. Holmes read the following Poem: —

OUR FIRST CITIZEN.

WINTER'S cold drift lies glistening o'er his breast;
  For him no spring shall bid the leaf unfold;
What Love could speak, by sudden grief oppressed,
  What swiftly summoned Memory tell, is told.

Even as the bells, in one consenting chime,
  Filled with their sweet vibrations all the air,
So joined all voices, in that mournful time,
  His genius, wisdom, virtues, to declare.

What place is left for words of measured praise,
  Till calm-eyed History, with her iron pen,
Grooves in the unchanging rock the final phrase
  That shapes his image in the souls of men?

Yet while the echoes still repeat his name,
  While countless tongues his full-orbed life rehearse,
Love, by his beating pulses taught, will claim
  The breath of song, the tuneful throb of verse, —

Verse that, in ever-changing ebb and flow,
　Moves, like the laboring heart, with rush and rest,
Or swings in solemn cadence, sad and slow,
　Like the tired heaving of a grief-worn breast.

This was a mind so rounded, so complete, —
　No partial gift of Nature in excess, —
That, like a single stream where many meet,
　Each separate talent counted something less.

A little hillock, if it lonely stand,
　Holds o'er the fields an undisputed reign,
While the broad summit of the table-land
　Seems with its belt of clouds a level plain.

Servant of all his powers, that faithful slave,
　Unsleeping Memory, strengthening with his toils,
To every ruder task his shoulder gave,
　And loaded every day with golden spoils.

Order, the law of Heaven, was throned supreme
　O'er action, instinct, impulse, feeling, thought;
True as the dial's shadow to the beam,
　Each hour was equal to the charge it brought.

Too large his compass for the nicer skill
　That weighs the world of science grain by grain;
All realms of knowledge owned the mastering will
　That claimed the franchise of his whole domain.

Earth, air, sea, sky, the elemental fire,
　Art, history, song, — what meanings lie in each
Found in his cunning hand a stringless lyre,
　And poured their mingling music through his speech.

Thence flowed those anthems of our festal days,
 Whose ravishing division held apart
The lips of listening throngs in sweet amaze,
 Moved in all breasts the self-same human heart.

Subdued his accents, as of one who tries
 To press some care, some haunting sadness down;
His smile half shadow; and to stranger eyes
 The kingly forehead wore an iron crown.

He was not armed to wrestle with the storm,
 To fight for homely truth with vulgar power;
Grace looked from every feature, shaped his form, —
 The rose of Academe, — the perfect flower!

Such was the stately scholar whom we knew
 In those ill days of soul-enslaving calm,
Before the blast of Northern vengeance blew
 Her snow-wreathed pine against the Southern palm.

Ah, God forgive us! did we hold too cheap
 The heart we might have known, but would not see,
And look to find the nation's friend asleep
 Though the dread hour of her Gethsemane?

That wrong is past; we gave him up to Death
 With all a hero's honors round his name;
As martyrs coin their blood, he coined his breath,
 And dimmed the scholar's in the patriot's fame.

So shall we blazon on the shaft we raise, —
 Telling our grief, our pride, to unborn years, —
"He who had lived the mark of all men's praise
 Died with the tribute of a nation's tears."

The Hon. Richard H. Dana then spoke as follows : —

MR. PRESIDENT : This full tide of grief and admiration
has carried along with it all there is of eulogy, and there
seems nothing left for me to-night — not wishing to say
over what has been so well said — but a single, commonplace suggestion, exciting no feeling, and entirely below
the demands of the hour. I would simply remind you,
brethren, that the fame of Mr. Everett has been fairly
earned.

It seems to me that he has earned his fame as fairly as
the painter, the poet, the sculptor, and the composer earn
theirs. The artist submits his picture or statue, the
composer his oratorio, and the poet his epic or lyric to
the . judgment of time, and abides the result. Mr.
Everett, for fifty years, year by year, submitted to the
judgment of his age orations, essays, lectures, speeches,
and diplomatic letters, and abided the result. If the
judgment has been favorable to him, what can have been
more fairly earned?

It has not only been earned without fraud on the public
judgment, or mistake or accident, but it has been earned
in strict compliance with the primeval law of labor— that
in the sweat of the brow all bread shall be eaten. It has
not been the result of a few happy strokes of genius. He
never did anything except with all the might his mind
and body could lend to it. He was first scholar at Harvard, because four years of competition left him so. If
he was in anything more learned than other men, it was
because he did his best with great natural powers. No

occasions occurred to him that may not occur to all. What other men made little of, he made everything of. He never trusted to genius or to chance. He owes as little, too, as any man, to the posts he has filled. Many derive importance from holding offices that connect them with great events. He stands upon his work, irrespective of office; and, indeed, his best and brightest acts have been those of a private citizen. Yes, brethren, every stone in the monument he has builded to himself has been quarried, fashioned, and polished by his own hand and eye.

Fairly earned, his fame is also firmly fixed. His style of thought and expression in written address has been tried by the tests of novelty and of familiarity, of sameness and of variety, in old communities and in new communities; and that style which forty years before, in its freshness, charmed the choice spirits of a critical community of readers and scholars, was found in its maturity, nay, almost in its age, equal to the conflict with the trained diplomatists of Europe, before the forum of nations.

So of his elocution. An orator may, by accidental charm of voice or manner, or by tricks of speech, gain celebrity for a time; but the crucial test comes, and he is found wanting, or he palls and stales by mere custom. But Mr. Everett's style of speech has been tried by every test, applied to every variety of topic, in different countries, and has survived the changes and chances of taste and opinion, as potent with the sons and daughters as with their fathers and mothers. At threescore and ten the spell of his elocution was as effective as in the freshness of his youth or the vigor of his manhood. The eloquence which forty and fifty years ago filled Brattle Street Church to the window-tops, which, in its new-born beauty, charmed the select assemblages at Cambridge, Concord, and Plymouth, was found in its gray and bent age, equal — more equal than any other — to the exigencies and shocks of the most vast and momentous popular canvass the world ever knew.

The Hon. B. F. Thomas spoke as follows : —

MR. PRESIDENT: If I had consulted my own judgment only, it would have been to listen to the gentlemen around me, the early, the life-long companions of the illustrious dead. I may not claim to have been of Mr. Everett's intimate friends. Though I have met him occasionally in private life, my means of knowledge are, after all, those of a reader and hearer of his public discourse. Nor have I, during a portion of his public life, been drawn to him by ties of political affinity and sympathy. Possibly, following the courtesies of parliamentary assemblies, these considerations may have led to the request that I should say a word this evening.

If the object of these services of commemoration were indiscriminate eulogy, the custom were more honored in the breach than in the observance ; such service being good neither for the dead nor the living. If we had no higher or nobler purpose, we might well turn to the pressing duties of life and of the hour, and let the dead bury their dead.

But if we believe the saying of an old historian, cited by Bolingbroke, that history is philosophy teaching by examples; if, rejecting the godless speculations of Buckle, we recognize in history the power and influence of the individual spirit; if we see in the lives of great and good men not only beacon lights on the line of human progress, but the most efficient of motive powers, the *causæ causantes;* that great and good men not only make history, but constitute history, and the best part of history; no work can be more appropriate to an historical society than the commemoration of such a life.

As you well observed, Mr. President, the other day in Faneuil Hall, in a speech, let me say, so worthy of its theme, one knows hardly where to begin or where to end. If we had but one word to say, it would be perhaps that Mr. Everett was the most *accomplished* man our country had produced; of the widest, most varied and finished culture. That using the word "orator," in the sense in which it has come to us from classic times, he was our most finished "orator," in fertility of resources, in aptness of use in grace of manner, in compass and music of voice, in curious felicity of diction, seldom if ever surpassed. Not always evincing magnetic power or projectile force, or the *ars artium celare artem ;* but in his best and happiest moods recalling the lines in which Milton, with such marvellous beauty, has described Adam, wrapt, entranced with the last accents that fell from the lips of Raphael : —

> "The angel ended; but in Adam's ear
> So charming left his voice that he awhile
> Thought him still speaking — still stood fixed to hear."

Though it was as a graceful and eloquent orator that
Mr. Everett was most widely known to his day and generation, we feel that in saying this we have not got very near
to our subject; that we have not touched upon the lines of
character which make the life of a great or good man the
worthy subject of study and contemplation.

Outside of revelation, Mr. President, men make their
own gods. They project them from within. They clothe
them with their own passions, they dwarf them by their
own infirmities. So it is in the construction of our heroes
and great men. We not only admire chiefly the qualities
in which we discover some resemblance to our own; but
we are very apt to dwell on them as the salient points of
character. We insist upon casting men into the moulds
of our own minds. This may be natural, but it is neither
manly nor just. That only is a manly and catholic criticism which appreciates and admires qualities utterly
diverse from our own; which recollects that our antipodes
stand also on the solid earth; that there may be diversities
of gifts but the same spirit, differences of administration
but the same Lord; that the eye cannot say to the hand,
I have no need of thee, nor the head to the feet, I have
no need of you; that this diversity of gifts and tendencies
is part of God's economy for the well-being and progress
of the race.

It is by the conflict and balance of forces that the plan-
ets know their places and "each in his motion like an
angel sings." A like conflict and balance of forces is the
law of human life and progress. In the shallow philosophy of Pope, there is not a shallower commonplace, than

" Just as the twig is bent the tree's inclined." You may twist and distort the growth of the tree, you may prune it into fantastic shapes, but the tree as God meant it to be lies wrapt in the germ, before the warm embrace of earth sends it up to greet the sun. The natural differences of men overcome and outgrow all culture and discipline. These two sons of the same parents, bred at the same fireside, trained in the same schools, surrounded by the same influences, ripened into manhood, the one shall become in politics a radical, the other a conservative. In religion one shall be the most protesting of protestants, the other repose with a child's trust on the bosom of the church.

In all free governments political parties are formed, and though they spring up sometimes for local and temporary purposes, yet as a general fact and in their last analysis, they will be found to be radical and conservative, the one having progress as its constant aim, the other dwelling upon the limitations of progress.

In the best sense of the word Mr. Everett was a conservative. No man more thoroughly understood or more fully appreciated the free institutions which the toils and sacrifices of good and wise and true men of twenty generations had secured to us. He had faith that whatever of error and imperfection was to be found in the work of the fathers would be removed by peaceful methods, by the progress of science, and art, and Christian culture and civilization. With his conservatism was found a broad, liberal, and catholic spirit. Bred in the extreme school of Protestantism, he did not understand by liberal Christianity the negation of things divine, the bowing of

religion out of the circle of the human mind. He did
not exclude from his idea of mental liberty the " liberty
of obedience ; " the liberty with which Christ makes men
free.

Bred in the school of the Puritans, illustrating their
virtues, admiring their sublime devotion to duty, he could
not have loved Puritanism the less because it was associated with the venerable past, because time had softened
and hallowed its more rugged features, because distance
lent enchantment to the view.

Bred in a school of politics, which, though of the highest integrity, had strong sectional tendencies, he was
among the most national of our statesmen. No part of
the land was shut out from his sympathy and regard.
His patriotism covered the country, however bounded.
No word dropped from his lips or pen to promote sectional hate or strife. His public life was a ministry of
concord and peace. He understood the compromises of
the Constitution, and was ready faithfully to abide by
them. He appreciated and admired this marvellous frame
of government, by which, for the first time in history,
central power was reconciled with local independence, the
immunities of free States with the capacities of a great
empire. From the first to the last, through evil report
and through good report, he clung to the Union of these
States and to the Constitution as its only bond. No man
labored more earnestly and devotedly to avert the coming
strife. His dread of civil conflict seemed to wear at times
almost the aspect of timidity. But if he felt more strongly
it was because he foresaw more clearly.

No greater injustice can be done to Mr. Everett, than by the suggestion that in the last three or four years of his life his opinions had undergone a radical change, and that the services of the past three years were a sort of propitiation and atonement for those that had gone before. Some of the views of public policy developed by Mr. Everett within the last two years did not command my assent. That was equally true with some of his earlier opinions. But I can see no necessary conflict between Mr. Everett the conservative statesman, the life-long defender of the Union and the Constitution, and Mr. Everett the ardent supporter of a war to secure from destruction that Union and Constitution. Difference of judgment as to what might be effected by force of arms might be the result of changes in the condition of the country, in the unity of sentiment and action in the loyal States. What seemed to him impossible in 1861, might, from the success of our arms, seem feasible in 1864. So measures that he deemed to be impolitic at the first period might seem to him to be demanded by the necessities of the second. Those differences marked no radical change of principles; and one, who differed from him on some few questions of policy while adhering to his general views, may be pardoned a word to save him from the too great kindness of his later friends.

Honor, as the heart shall prompt, his labors to uphold the arm of government against secession, to give unity to its counsels and efforts, to bring all men to its standard. We may honor none the less a life given to what his nephew and my friend has fitly called the ministry of

conciliation, to the victories of peace. Nor will we forget
how, at the first glimpse of opportunity, he turned to his
first love; how, when the cry of suffering came from a
conquered city, his heart went out to meet and to help it;
how naturally he recurred to the power of Christian sympathies and kindness; how the blessed words of the
royal preacher of Israel sprung to his lips, "If thine
enemy hunger, feed him; if he thirst, give him drink."

Blessed close of a great and good life. Blessed privilege to forget for a moment the horrors and glories even
of war, the shouts and waving banners of triumph, to sit
again at the feet of the Divine Master, to lean upon his
bosom, to be kindled by and to radiate his divine love.

Hon. James Savage made the following remarks : —

Mr. PRESIDENT: I am a little surprised to be called up;
and yet, sir, as the catalogue of the Society shows, Mr.
Everett's name stood next to mine, I hope I may be excused if the infirmity of age is more apparent than anything else in what I say. I can refer to the early days of
Mr. Everett, which has not been more than once alluded
to, and that before he had adopted the resolution of taking
the profession of a preacher of the Everlasting Gospel.
In this he was most eminently successful, and before that
I remember well, sir, that the boy was father to the man.

No one who then looked at him and heard him, would
have failed to foretell the success which attended him. Of
Mr. Everett, I suppose it can be said as of other men,
that he touched nothing that he did not adorn. I cannot

give you the Latin, sir, but it is one of the very strong illustrations of human grace and felicity. It was very observable. When I was in England I had the advantage of great attention from Mr. Everett. When their chief statesman, Sir Robert Peel, was suddenly stricken down by instant death — and when the Earl of Aberdeen, another great friend of our country, succeeded him, continuing to maintain all our just rights consistent with the rights of his own country, — I had the advantage of meeting at Mr. Everett's, more than once or twice, some of the first gentlemen of England, chiefly official persons, and there to observe that no man of their own country was more attended to or less inclined to presume upon that attention. He seemed to be always the servant of the public in private as well as in public. I believe that our country has never had a superior minister anywhere at any court. I only wish that our present representative, my younger friend, may make Mr. Everett's place good.

Hon. Emory Washburn addressed the meeting as follows: —

Mr. President: I shall not presume, in such a presence, to speak of Mr. Everett as a scholar, for I should feel that, by so doing, I was trespassing upon ground which would be so much more properly occupied by others. Nor will the time allotted me, admit of my dwelling upon the prominent part which he has taken in the historic events of the last thirty years of his life.

On the other hand, I cannot pretend to that intimate relation in the associations with him with which I have been favored, which would justify my attempting to draw

the nicer shades of character which intimacy alone en-
ables one to analyze and trace. The most I can hope to
do, is to give, in general terms, the results upon my own
mind of the observation of more than forty years, chiefly,
of his public life. And yet I have too often shared in
his acts of personal kindness and courtesy, not to feel that
I have a right to speak, also, of some of those traits of
private character which stand out so prominently in the
history of his life.

The impression which my study and observation of Mr.
Everett's career have left most strongly defined upon my
own mind, is its harmony and completeness in all its parts
and characteristic qualities. In no field of honor or usefulness which he was called upon to occupy, did he ever
fail to meet its reasonable requirements, nor did he ever
shrink from the labor which its duties imposed. Many
men have been great in one department of intellectual
power or excellence, without possessing any claims to
distinction in any other. Some cultivate one set of their
powers or faculties, at the expense of the others. And of
many, the judgments which we form, are but the balancing of one quality against another, the good against the
evil, in order to ascertain at what point in the scale of
moral worth we are to place them, in the estimate which
we form of their character. The great warrior may be
the brutal tyrant or the sordid miser. The brilliant poet
may not soar above the atmosphere of his own vices, and
the splendid orator while arousing and wielding the passions of others, at his will, may be the veriest slave of
his own. Examples like these serve to mark the contrast

of good and evil which are found in so many of the men
whom the world has called famous.

But in the life of Mr. Everett, we seek, in vain, for any
such contrasts as these. It was not because there were
not, in the constitution of his mind and character, prominent
and striking qualities, but because there was no occasion
to go through the process of balancing these qualities
against each other, in order to determine the relative rank
of merit in which he is hereafter to be held in the judgment
of posterity. His character in this respect was homoge-
neous in its elements, and complete, as well in its parts, as
in the relations of these to each other.

That which must have struck every one who knew Mr.
Everett as worthy of special notice, was the *filling up*, if I
may so say, which gave to his life and character that
roundness of proportion which renders it difficult, as we
now look upon it, to say which of the traits for which he
was distinguished, stand out most prominently upon the
canvas. The picture is therefore in danger of being
indistinct, from the absence of shade by which to bring
out its features into bolder relief. He was the scholar at
the same time that he was the orator of the pulpit and of
the senate. He was the statesman and the diplomatist,
the administrative officer, and, for many years of his life,
the leading citizen in all the land. He was the Christian
gentleman and the patriot; — and he won in them all, the
respect and admiration of the country. And yet, who is
now ready to say in which of these he transcended his
own excellence in any other trait into which his character
may be divided? Had he been either of these alone,

there would have been, in the graces and accomplishments which he would have brought to its duties, enough
to have given to his life in that sphere, the seeming
finish of completeness. This is what I mean by that
filling up which gave such an admirable fulness and
consistency of proportion, in his character and life.

I might illustrate this thought further by referring to
what is familiar, perhaps, to us all. It is more than forty
years since I first heard him in the pulpit. I need not
say with how much delight I listened to the rich and
varied thought, the beauty of diction, the inimitable power
of description, the affluence of illustration, and the pathos
of appeal which gave so much life to his sermons of that
day. These qualities of high pulpit oratory may not
have been peculiar to him. But there was added to
these, a beauty of countenance, a grace in action, a
sweetness in voice, and an impressive, though almost
measured modulation in tone and cadence, which left
upon the mind of the hearer the conviction that he was
unsurpassed as a rhetorician and an orator.

I afterwards heard him on the floor of Congress, and
there he was no less at home than in the pulpit. And
the dignity of his bearing, the mastery he showed of his
subject, and the eloquence of the language he uttered,
commanded the willing attention of that body, while it
was yet dignified by men of eloquence and a national
fame.

We all know how faithfully and conscientiously he
performed the duties of the Executive of this Commonwealth. Nothing was left undone which courtesy, or

kindness, or etiquette, claimed at his hand, from patiently
listening to the broken language of the wife or mother
pleading for the pardon of a wayward husband or son, to
those dignified state papers which came from his pen
perfect in all their parts. The same may be said of the
manner in which he bore himself at the court of St.
James, and as successor of Mr. Webster, at the head of
our American court at Washington.

And in this, I do not mean to refer so much to great
exhibitions of skill and power as a diplomatist and a
statesman, as to the qualities which belonged to him personally as a man, and which helped to grace and fill up
the measure of his official character.

But this character for completeness to which I have
alluded, may perhaps be better illustrated in the personal
qualities which he exhibited in the amenities of private
life. We have heard him called cold in his sympathies,
and ungenial of manners, in his intercourse with others;
and I confess that, till I knew him, I thought his seeming
reserved, if not austere. But I need not say, in this
presence, how soon this impression was corrected when
one came in direct contact with him, either socially, or in
the ordinary intercourse of private life. There was in
his organization something of that shrinking delicacy
which makes one apparently shy and sensitive. But I
will venture to say, that no one ever went to him for
kindness, or sympathy, or counsel, and found him either
cold or repulsive.

He never forgot the courtesies of the gentleman in his
intercourse with any man, however humble or devoid of

influence he may have been. He never was surpassed in
the scrupulous punctuality with which he replied to a
correspondent, however unimportant the subject addressed
to him, nor in the indulgence with which he received
and the kindness with which he acknowledged, the well
intended but often equivocal favor of printed works and
papers, with which authors loaded his table and taxed his
time — the thing he was the least able to spare.

The kindliness of his nature was manifested in a
hundred different forms, though rarely so as to attract the
observation or applause of others. In all the trying situa-
tions in which he was placed, at times, censured by party
antagonism, misconstrued in his motives and his acts, and
smarting under the keen rebuke of public disfavor, I do
not believe any one ever saw him lose the dignity of his
self possession, or heard him indulge in harsh or uncour-
teous language towards his bitterest opponent.

Nor will the world ever know how often the deserving
young man, struggling with adverse circumstances, has
found in him, what he needed more than money — a wise
counsellor and a kind friend. Hundreds could now tell
us how he sought them out, aided and encouraged them,
and helped them onward in a career of usefulness and
honor. While his body lay waiting for that august
solemnity in which a whole city, and, I might add, a State
and Nation bore a part, the door bell of his house was
rung, and, upon its being opened, there stood upon the
threshold a young man, a stranger, in the dress of a
junior officer in the navy. He asked permission to come
in and look, once more, upon the form and face of Mr.

Everett. " I am a stranger to you," said he to the gentleman in attendance, " but Mr. Everett was the best friend I ever had ; he procured me the place I now hold, and from that day has never failed to write me letters of en-couragement and advice, although I had no claim upon his kindness and generosity."

Of his affluence, whether of wisdom or learning, of worldly gifts or kindly consideration, he never withheld, when appealed to by objects of merit and desert.

I desire also to say a single word upon another error into which the public mind may have naturally fallen. Whatever he wrote or delivered was, uniformly, so finished and perfect in style and language, as well as in thought, that an impression became general that he had little ready or spontaneous eloquence, and that, in order to meet an occasion, he must have time for careful prepa-ration. In the danger which he had to contend with, of having himself for a rival, he was, undoubtedly, loth to speak without previous preparation. But his friends knew that he was not only a man of ready and stirring eloquence, but that, with all the grave, serious, and dig-nified manner which characterized so many of his orations and public addresses, he had a fund of keen and sprightly wit, of playful humor, and apt and gentle repartee, which, at times, electrified the hour, and delighted whoever was fortunate enough to witness them.

It might seem that for one who, through a long period of public services, had shown himself worthy to hold a place in the foremost rank, nothing could be needed to

fill up and round out a life of so much active usefulness
and honor.

But do we not all feel, now, how much it would have
wanted, if it had lacked the finish with which the history of
the last four years has crowned and completed the work?
Nobody had a right to doubt the honesty and sincerity of
his convictions and opinions, however much one may
have differed from him in the matters of public policy.
But he saw the coming of that dreadful storm which has
been sweeping over our country, and, like many other
true patriots, he was willing to avert it by a conciliatory
policy, though, by so doing, he subjected himself to the
imputation of timidity or want of heart. But when he
saw that the scheme of the conspirators was not to secure
the rights which were theirs, but to usurp those to which
they had no claim; when he saw that the purpose at
which they aimed was not peace, but the overthrow, by
war, of the Government under which our country had
grown great and prosperous and happy, he threw the full
weight of his accumulated power of intellect and influence into the struggle, and, in the forgetfulness of old
opinions and cherished associations, he gave up to his
country the stores of learning, the resources of eloquence,
and the gathered energies of an entire life devoted to
diligence and duty. Men no longer called him timid, for
he showed that he had that highest of all courage, which
dares to go against one's own prepossessions and uttered
opinions, when in the light of present events, he looks
back upon the unintentional mistakes of the past. The
nation, the world itself looked on with admiration, as this

brave old champion in the cause of right, urged on the battle by his trumpet call to duty and to arms. And they felt that his record was complete, his life rounded out into the full proportions of Christian manliness, when he uttered that last noble appeal, to crown the triumphs of a nation's success, by the divine magnanimity that feeds our enemy and carries him comfort in the hour of prostration and distress.

While standing upon that lofty eminence of fame, to which a long and arduous life of noble action had raised him, it was a kind Providence that spared him from even the possibility of danger of any coming misapprehension or mistake. He laid by his armor before the evening shadows had dimmed a single gleam of its brightness. But he went not to his rest till his last day's work was fully and nobly accomplished. He put off the garb which he had worn amid the dust and toil of an ever busy life, to waken to a new existence where, while the past is secure, the future can never be clouded by the passions of erring nature, or the frailties of human judgment.

The fame which, till then, had been in his own keeping, he left in charge of the country he had so long served. And can we doubt that the trust will be sacredly kept? They will rear to him statues and monuments. And they will do more. They will keep these monuments and memorials alive, by cherishing the memory of the man to whom they are reared, in the treasured offerings of a nation's history.

It will be but another illustration of the immortality

which the fame of a truly great man lends to the works
of art, by which men seek to perpetuate the memory of
the dead.   The chisel of the artist may bring out from
the marble the form and features of one whom pride or
affection may seek to honor.   But it is, at last, to history
that we must look, to interpret the record which sculp-
ture may have tried to register.

You, sir, beautifully reminded us, on another occasion,
of the search of the Roman orator amongst the rank
weeds and gathered rubbish of the cemetery of Syracuse,
for the forgotten monument of Archimedes, while you
reminded his countrymen that the great American Philos-
opher and Statesman, till then, had no memorial of art
reared to him, even in the city where he was born.
But though they answered that appeal with a generous
alacrity, the enduring bronze of which his speaking
statue is fashioned by the skilful cunning of art, would
do little to keep his memory alive for the service of posterity, if his name had not been enrolled among the great
names that shed lustre upon the pages of his country's
history.

So it will be with the statue which, as we trust, a
gratified people will place by the side of his great com-
patriot, in the front of our Capitol.   It is fitting that it
should stand there, a memorial, immortal in the light of
history, of the man, and of a people's gratitude.   The
name of Everett, repeated to the inquirer in after ages,
will reanimate that form, and it will speak of the scholar,
the statesman, the orator, the patriot, and the Christian

gentleman, to whom it shall have been reared by a people that knew, and loved, and honored him.

The Rev. Mr. Waterston read the following communication from John G. Whittier, introducing the letter by the words of Dr. Channing, who said of Mr. Whittier, more than a quarter of a century ago: " His poetry bursts from the soul with the fire and energy of an ancient prophet. And his noble simplicity of character is the delight of all who know him."

AMESBURY, 27th 1st Month, 1865.

MY DEAR FRIEND: I acknowledge through thee, the invitation of the standing committee of the Massachusetts Historical Society to be present at a special meeting of the Society for the purpose of paying a tribute to the memory of our late illustrious associate, Edward Everett.

It is a matter of deep regret to me that the state of my health will not permit me to be with you on an occasion of so much interest.

It is most fitting that the members of the Historical Society of Massachusetts should add their tribute to those which have been already offered by all sects, parties, and associations, to the name and fame of their late associate. He was himself a maker of history, and part and parcel of all the noble charities and humanizing influences of his State and time.

When the grave closed over him who added new lustre to the old and honored name of Quincy, all eyes instinctively turned to Edward Everett as the last of that venerated class of patriotic civilians who, outliving all dissent and jealousy and party prejudice, held their reputation

by the secure tenure of the universal appreciation of its
worth as a common treasure of the republic. It is not
for me to pronounce his eulogy. Others, better qualified
by their intimate acquaintance with him, have done and
will do justice to his learning, eloquence, varied culture,
and social virtues. My secluded country life has afforded
me few opportunities of personal intercourse with him,
while my pronounced radicalism, on the great question
which has divided popular feeling, rendered our political
paths widely divergent. Both of us early saw the danger
which threatened the country. In the language of the
prophet, we " saw the sword coming upon the land," but
while he believed in the possibility of averting it by
concession and compromise, I, on the contrary, as firmly
believed that such a course could only strengthen and
confirm what I regarded as a gigantic conspiracy against
the rights and liberties, the union and the life, of the
nation.

Recent events have certainly not tended to change this
belief on my part; but in looking over the past, while I
see little or nothing to retract in the matter of opinion, I
am saddened by the reflection, that through the very
intensity of my convictions I may have done injustice to
the motives of those with whom I differed. As respects
Edward Everett, it seems to me that only within the last
four years I have truly known him.

In that brief period, crowded as it is with a whole
life-work of consecration to the union, freedom, and
glory of his country, he not only commanded respect
and reverence, but concentrated upon himself in a most

remarkable degree the love of all loyal and generous
hearts. We have seen, in these years of trial, very great
sacrifices offered upon the altar of patriotism — wealth,
ease, home-love, life itself. But Edward Everett did
more than this; he laid on that altar not only his time,
talents, and culture, but his pride of opinion, his long-
cherished views of policy, his personal and political
predilections and prejudices, his constitutional fastidious-
ness of conservatism, and the carefully elaborated sym-
metry of his public reputation. With a rare and noble
magnanimity, he met, without hesitation, the demand of
the great occasion. Breaking away from all the beset-
ments of custom and association, he forgot the things that
are behind, and, with an eye single to present duty,
pressed forward towards the mark of the high calling of
Divine Providence in the events of our time. All honor
to him! If we mourn that he is now beyond the reach
of our poor human praise, let us reverently trust that he
has received that higher plaudit: "Well done, thou good
and faithful servant!"

When I last met him, as my colleague in the Electoral
College of Massachusetts, his look of health and vigor
seemed to promise us many years of his wisdom and
usefulness. On greeting him I felt impelled to express
my admiration and grateful appreciation of his patriotic
labors; and I shall never forget how readily and grace-
fully he turned attention from himself to the great cause
in which we had a common interest, and expressed his
thankfulness that he had still a country to serve.

To keep green the memory of such a man is at once a

privilege and a duty.   That stainless life of seventy years
is a priceless legacy.   His hands were pure.   The shadow
of suspicion never fell on him.   If he erred in his
opinions (and that he did so, he had the Christian grace
and courage to own), no selfish interest weighed in the
scale of his judgment against truth.

As our thoughts follow him to his last resting-place,
we are sadly reminded of his own touching lines, written
many years ago at Florence.   The name he has left
behind is none the less " pure " that instead of being
" humble," as he then anticipated, it is on the lips of
grateful millions, and written ineffaceably on the record
of his country's trial and triumph : —

> " Yet not for me when I shall fall asleep
> Shall Santa Croce's lamps their vigils keep ;
> Beyond the main in Auburn's quiet shade,
> With those I loved and love my couch be made ; —
> Spring's pendent branches o'er the hillock wave,
> And morning's dewdrops glisten on my grave,
> While Heaven's great arch shall rise above my bed,
> When Santa Croce's crumbles on her dead —
> Unknown to erring or to suffering fame,
> So I may leave a pure though humble name "

Congratulating the Society on the prospect of the speedy
consummation of the great objects of our associate's
labors—the peace and permanent union of our country.—

I am very truly thy friend,

JOHN G. WHITTIER

ROBERT C. WATERSTON, BOSTON.

The meeting then adjourned.

www.ingramcontent.com/pod-product-compliance
Lightning Source LLC
Chambersburg PA
CBHW020303090426
42735CB00009B/1195